Washington County,

—AND THE—

EARLY SETTLEMENT OF OHIO.

Washington County,

— AND THE —

EARLY SETTLEMENT OF OHIO.

BEING THE

Centennial Historical Address,

BEFORE THE CITIZENS OF WASHINGTON COUNTY,

—BY—

ISRAEL WARD ANDREWS, LL. D.,

President of Marietta College.

MARIETTA, OHIO, JULY 4th, 1876.

CINCINNATI:
PETER G. THOMSON, PUBLISHER, 179 VINE STREET,
1877.

Copyright © 2023 by Commonwealth Book Company, Inc.

All rights reserved. No part of this book may be reproduced in any form or by any means without the prior written consent of the publisher, excepting brief quotes used in reviews. Printed in the United States of America.

ISBN: 978-1-948986-53-3

CORRESPONDENCE.

SECRETARY'S OFFICE
WASHINGTON CO., AGRICULTURAL & MECHANICAL ASS'N.

Marietta, O., Feb. 19th, 1876.

I. W. ANDREWS, D. D.,

Dear Sir:—The Board of Directors of the Washington County Agricultural and Mechanical Association, at a meeting held Feb. 16th, 1876, in conformity with the recommendations of the Centennial authorities at Philadelphia, and the Annual Agricultural Convention of this State, and to carry such recommendations into effect, selected you to prepare and deliver an historical address the coming Fourth of July. It would afford me pleasure to receive your acceptance.

Yours most respectfully,

C. T. FRAZYER,
Secretary.

Marietta College, Feb. 22, 1876.

Dear Sir:—I have the honor to acknowledge the receipt of your letter of the 19th instant, conveying to me an invitation from the "Washington County Agricultural and Mechanical Association," to prepare and deliver, on the Fourth of July next, an historical address pertaining to the development of the county within the century.

Will you convey to the Board of Directors my appreciation of the honor conferred on me in selecting me for this service, and my grateful acceptance of the same?

Yours truly,

ISRAEL W. ANDREWS.

HON. C. T. FRAZYER, *Secretary, &c.*

Correspondence.

At a subsequent meeting of citizens, the following officers were appointed for the celebration of the Centennial Fourth of July:

Hon. P. B. BUELL, *President.*

Vice Presidents.—Adams, S. N. Merriam; Aurelius, J. D. James; Barlow, D. N. Dunsmore; Belpre, L. E. Stone; Decatur, A. Russell; Dunham, S. D. Ellenwood; Fairfield, C. H. Goddard; Fearing, Chas. Zimmer; Grandview, Jasper Lisk; Harmar, Col. D. Barber; Independence, August Hille; Lawrence, A. J. Dye; Liberty, John Congleton; Ludlow, Isaac Scott; Marietta—1st Ward, Wm. Glines; 2d, Jewett Palmer; 3d, I. R. Waters; Marietta Tp., W. F. Curtis; Muskingum, L. J. P. Putnam; Newport, J. B. Greene; Palmer, J. M. Murdock; Salem, Walter Thomas; Union, Matthew Jurden; Warren, C. B. Tuttle; Waterford, H. F. Devol; Watertown, Isaac Johnson; Wesley, B. F. Arnold.

Col. T. W. MOORE, *Marshal.*

Reading of the *Declaration of Independence,* Capt. W. H. GURLEY.

On the 25th of May, President Grant issued a Proclamation bringing to the notice of the people, a joint resolution of Congress, recommending their assembling in their several counties and towns on the Centennial Anniversary, and " that they cause to have delivered on such day, an historical sketch of said county or town, and that a copy of said sketch may be filed, in print or manuscript, in the Clerk's office of the said county, and an additional copy be filed in the office of the Librarian of Congress, to the intent that a complete record may thus be obtained of the progress of our institutions during the first Centennial of their existence."

In accordance with this recommendation and the arrangements previously made, the citizens of Washington County, assembled at Marietta, and duly celebrated the Centennial Anniversary of our National Independence.

Hon. P. B. Buell presided, and Col. T. W. Moore officiated as marshal. Prayer was offered by Rev. S. C. Frampton, and the Declaration of Independence was read by William H. Gurley, Esq. The historical address was then delivered by the orator of the day.

Historical Address.

FELLOW CITIZENS OF WASHINGTON COUNTY: On this day, one hundred years ago, the Thirteen United Colonies became THE UNITED STATES OF AMERICA. The people of the colonies, through their representatives in General Congress assembled, publicly declared themselves absolved from all allegiance to the British Crown, and solemnly and religiously proclaimed to the world their determination to assume and maintain a separate and equal station among the nations of the earth. It was a bold declaration to be made by those small and feeble colonies, against a great and powerful nation. But they believed in the justness of their cause and could appeal to the Supreme Judge of the world for the rectitude of their intentions. They placed a firm reliance on the protection of Divine Providence; and the more we study our national history from that eventful day to this, the clearer are the proofs that that protection has not been withheld.

There is not need to recount the steps by which our fathers were led to dissolve the bonds that bound the colonies to the mother country. The first meeting to consider their grievances, was in 1765, when delegates from nine colonies met in New York. The passage of the Stamp Act by Parliament, in March of that year, was the immediate occasion of this Congress. They adopted a declaration of rights and claimed the treatment due to British subjects: "that it is inseparably essential to the freedom of a people, and the undoubted right of Englishmen, that no taxes be imposed on them but with their own consent, given personally or by their representatives." This sentiment passed into a maxim, "taxation without representation is tyranny." If Parliament should enact laws to tax the people of the colonies, the representatives of the colonies ought to be admitted as members of Parliament. The maxim did not mean that taxation without suffrage is tyranny, for the ordinance for this north-west territory provided that no one could vote without "a freehold in fifty acres of land in the district."

The Stamp Act was repealed, but other taxes and duties were imposed quite as obnoxious to the colonies. In September, 1774, the first Continental Congress met at Philadelphia, embracing delegates from twelve colonies. There were men in that Congress whose names have become household words. Addresses to the king, to the people of Great Britain, to the people of the colonies, and to the inhabitants of the Province of Quebec, were drawn up, and the Congress hoped that their grievances would be redressed. But should the course of the king continue as before, they recommended a second Congress in the month of May following. The king remained obstinate, and the second Continental Congress was convened as had been recommended. But hostilities had already commenced at Lexington and Concord, and measures for defense were immediately taken. An army was organized, and on the 15th of June George

The Declaration of Independence.

Washington was unanimously elected general of all the forces. His commission styled him the "General and Commander-in-Chief of the Army of the United Colonies."

The breach became wider and wider. The people began to talk of separation. On the 7th of June, 1776, Richard Henry Lee, in accordance with the vote of the Virginia Convention, moved in Congress a declaration of independence. After a most thorough discussion in the committee of the whole it was adopted on the tenth. The further consideration was postponed till July. On the second of that month it was adopted in Congress; and on the fourth the declaration, which had been prepared by a committee previously appointed, was adopted. While the resolution was passed on the second, the formal declaration was adopted on the fourth, and thus that became our national birth-day. Each of the colonies was transformed into a State, and the thirteen united colonies became an independent nation. Whether the independence thus declared could be maintained was to be decided by the sword. Should the people fail in the great struggle, they would have no place as a nation on the page of history. Should they succeed, their national existence would date from the fourth of July, 1776.

We celebrate the one hundredth anniversary of that day. The American Republic has completed her first century. It has been a century of growth. From about three millions of people we have become more than forty millions. From a little strip along the Atlantic coast our possessions have increased till they extend from ocean to ocean, and from the forty-ninth parallel of latitude to the gulf. Including Alaska, the territory now belonging to the United States is nearly ten times as large as that occupied by the thirteen colonies. The number of States has increased to thirty-seven, with Colorado to be admitted, probably during the present month; indeed considered already as a State by the great conventions of Cincinnati and St. Louis.[1]

The two great events of the century have been the formation and adoption of the Constitution of the United States, and the recent civil war. This great struggle, while it was a sectional war growing out of slavery as its immediate cause, was in reality a conflict of ideas— the old articles of confederation pitted against the constitution of 1787. Appeal was made to the arbitrament of the sword, and the doctrine of the government has been settled, as so many other great political questions have been, by blood. The institution of slavery is gone; those who were defeated in the great struggle accept the situation, and we may hope that all parts of the nation will be bound together by a closer tie, and that no root of bitterness will ever again spring up to trouble us.

The invitation with which I have been honored, to address my fellow citizens of Washington County on this Centennial Independence day, does not allow me to speak at length of national questions, or national progress; but confines me for the most part to what pertains to the origin and development of our own county.

It is an honor to be the orator on this day, for this, the oldest county in the great North-west, bearing the name of the one man whom all Americans hold in reverence; whose history, more than that of any other, is interwoven with the history of the State.

---

1. The proclamation of the President admitting Colorado was issued on the first of August, 1876.

Title of the United States to Ohio.

This region was originally a part of the vast district claimed by the French, and known as Louisiana. The Mississippi river was discovered by French missionaries, and was subsequently explored to its mouth by LaSalle, who, according to the custom of the nations of that day, took possession in the name of his sovereign, Louis XIV, of the vast region drained by its waters. After the French war, France, by the treaty of peace of 1763, ceded to Great Britain all her possessions east of the Mississippi river. When the war of the American Revolution broke out, the whole of the eastern part of the great Mississippi valley was claimed by Great Britain, and by the treaty of 1783 between that power and the United States this region was relinquished to our nation. It is true that various States of the Union laid claim during the Revolutionary war to large tracts west of the Alleghenies on the ground of old English charters, but their claims were conflicting and it was the policy of Congress not to decide between them. Eventually all these States made cessions of their claims, some with and others without reservations; but the probabilities are that the nation as a whole, which had really wrested the lands from Great Britain, was by the laws of nations the rightful owner of the region. These lands thus came from the French to the English by the treaty of 1763, and from the English to the United States by the treaty of 1783. And it is a pleasant coincidence that when General Rufus Putnam, in 1757, then only nineteen years old, and others of the noble pioneers of Ohio, shouldered their muskets and made those wearisome marches to Canada and endured such great privations in the old French war, they were really fighting for the region which was to be their future home, and where they were to lay the foundations of many rich and prosperous States.

The settlement at Marietta in 1788 grew out of an appropriation of lands made by Congress in 1776 to the officers and soldiers of the army. Those who should serve during the war were to receive tracts according to their rank; a Colonel 500 acres, a Lieutenant Colonel 450, and so on, a private soldier 100. In 1780 the act was extended to General officers; a Major-General to receive 1,100, a Brigadier-General 850. In June 1783, the officers of the army to the number of 288, petitioned Congress that the lands to which they were entitled might be located in " that tract of country bounded north on Lake Erie, east on Pennsylvania, south-east and south on the river Ohio, west on a line beginning at that part of the Ohio which lies twenty-four miles west of the mouth of the river Scioto, thence running north on a meridian line till it intersects the river Miami, which falls into Lake Erie, thence down the middle of that river to the Lake." They speak of this tract as " of sufficient extent, the land of such quality and situation, as may induce Congress to assign and mark it out as a tract or territory suitable to form a distinct government (or Colony of the United States), in time to be admitted one of the Confederated States of America;" and also as " a tract of country not claimed as the property of, or within the jurisdiction of, any particular State of the Union."

General Rufus Putnam forwarded this petition to General Washington, accompanying it with a long and able letter, in which he detailed the advantages which the establishment of such a colony would secure to the whole country. He says; " The part which I have taken in promoting the petition is well known, and therefore needs no apology when I inform you that the signers expect that I will pursue measures to have it laid before Congress; under these circumstances I beg leave to put the petition into your Excellency's hands, and ask with the greatest assurance your patronage of it." He suggests a chain of forts, say twenty miles apart, extending from the Ohio to the Lake by the Scioto or Muskingum. His letter concludes thus: "The petitioners conceive that sound policy dictates the measure, and that Congress ought to lose no time in establishing some such chains of forts as has been hinted at, and in procuring the tract of country petitioned for, of the natives; for the moment this is done, and agreeable terms offered to the settlers, many of the petitioners are determined, not only to become adventurers, but actually to remove themselves to this country; and there is not the least doubt but other valuable citizens will follow their example, and the probability is that the country between Lake Erie and the Ohio will be filled with inhabitants, and the faithful subjects of these United States so established on the waters of the Ohio and the lakes, as to banish forever the idea of our Western territory falling under the dominion of any European power, the frontiers of the old states will be effectually secured from savage alarms, and the new will have little to fear from their insults."

In this letter General Putnam speaks of townships six miles square, with reservations for the ministry and schools—probably the first suggestion of the kind. General Washington immediately transmits this petition, with a copy of General Putnam's letter, to the President of Congress, accompanying it with an earnest letter.

In April, 1784, General Putnam writes again to Washington, who in his reply expresses great regret at the inaction of Congress. He says, " for surely if justice and gratitude to the army, and general policy of the Union were to govern in this case, there would not be the smallest interruption in granting its request." [1]

In January, 1786, Generals Rufus Putnam and Benjamin Tupper issued a call for a meeting of officers and soldiers and others to form an Ohio Company. The meeting was held in Boston, March 1st, delegates being present from eight counties. General Putnam was the president of the meeting and Major Winthrop Sargent, clerk. A committee was appointed to prepare articles of association, and the Ohio Company of Associates was duly organized. The object was to raise a fund in continental certificates, for the sole purpose of buying western lands in the Western Territor; and making a settlement.

The fund was not to exceed a million dollars in continental specie certificates, exclusive of one year's interest, each share to consist of one thousand dollars in certificates and one year's interest; and ten dollars in gold or silver. This interest and the gold and silver were to be used for incidental charges, expenses of agents, &c. No person was to hold more than five shares. An agent represented twenty shares.

The officers were to be five directors, a treasurer, and a secretary, to be appointed by the agents. The directors were to have sole control of the Company's fund, and the lands purchased were to be divided by lot as the agents should direct.

1. This autograph letter of General Washington, dated 2d June, 1784, is among the Putnam papers in the library of Marietta College, presented by Hon. William R. Putnam, grandson of General Rufus Putnam.

The Ohio Company's Purchase.

Three directors were appointed in March, 1787: General Samuel H. Parsons, General Rufus Putnam and Reverend Doctor Manasseh Cutler. Major Winthrop Sargent, was made secretary. At a meeting in August, General James M. Varnum, of Rhode Island, was elected a director, and Richard Platt, of New York, treasurer. Doctor Cutler was employed to purchase of Congress land for the Company in the "Great Western Territory of the Union," and in July, 1787, went for that purpose to New York, where the Continental Congress was then in session.

The year 1787 was an eventful year. The present Constitution of the United States was framed, the ordinance for the government of the Territory North-west of the River Ohio was enacted, and the purchase of land was made by the Ohio Company. The North American Review for April of this year says: "The ordinance of 1787, and the Ohio purchase were parts of one and the same transaction. The purchase *would* not have been made without the ordinance, and the ordinance *could* not have been enacted except as an essential condition of the purchase."

The contract was made for 1,500,000 acres, Congress passing an act to that effect July 27th, acceding to the terms proposed by Doctor Cutler; the ordinance for the Territory having been passed on the 13th of the month.

This is the place to speak particularly of two men in connection with this settlement. Many of the early settlers were eminent men. No other settlement of modern times can show so many—but two were especially prominent, *General Rufus Putnam* and *Doctor Manasseh Cutler.*

Centennial Historical Address.

General Putnam early conceived the idea of an organized emigration to the West. He wrote to Washington in 1783, and again in 1784: he had previously, in 1773, explored West Florida with reference to grants from the British Government for those who had served in the French War. He presided at the meeting called to form the Ohio Company, and was chairman of the committee to draft the articles of association. He was one of the three directors first appointed, and after the purchase he was appointed Superintendent of all the business of the company relating to the settlement of the lands. He was at once appointed a Judge of the Court of Common Pleas, very soon was made one of the three Judges of the Territory, and later became the Surveyor-General of the United States. Before coming to Ohio he had risen from the position of a common soldier to the rank of Brigadier-General. He had the confidence of Washington. In every position in which he was placed he succeeded. By the force of his character, by his integrity, his energy, he accomplished whatever he undertook. It is impossible to study the history of those times and the part he acted without being impressed with the solidity and excellence of his character, intellectual and executive, moral and religious. In a community of able men, many of them highly educated, General Putnam was from the first the leading man.

Doctor Cutler was not among the pioneers, though his children were; his connection and agency were especially in the purchase of the land, and in framing the ordinance of 1787. He was a highly cultivated man, a graduate of Yale College, and a member of divers philosophical societies. At that time he was pastor of a church in Eastern Massachusetts. He was at the meeting, March

1st, 1786, was placed on the committee to draft articles, all the others being military men, and was made a director with General Putnam and General Parsons. He was appointed to purchase the land, and while making the negotiation the ordinance of 1787 was enacted.

An ordinance for the North-west Territory had been reported in Congress in March, 1784, by a committee of which Mr. Jefferson was chairman. It prohibited slavery after 1800, but this restricting clause was stricken out. It was passed April 23d, and remained on the statute book till repealed by the ordinance of 1787. Various efforts had been made to improve it, but without success.

Dr. Cutler reached New York July 5th. On the 9th a new committee on the ordinance was appointed. On the 11th the ordinance was reported, and on the 13th it was passed, with but one vote against it. No act of legislation by any legislative body in the United States has been more highly praised than this. Mr. Webster says: "We are accustomed to praise the law-givers of antiquity; we help to perpetuate the fame of Solon and Lycurgus; but I doubt whether one single law of any law-giver, ancient or modern, has produced effects of more distinct, marked, and lasting character than the ordinance of 1787."

Judge Timothy Walker says: "It approaches as near to absolute perfection as anything to be found in the legislation of mankind."

For this immortal ordinance we are largely, perhaps chiefly, indebted to Dr Cutler. The evidence of his agency in it has been recently re-examined and presented by a writer in the North American Review, and it seems to be unanswerable. This ordinance was the first under which any Territory was organized, and it has been the model for all those that have since been enacted.

How great the obligations of the great North-west and of the whole country are to this quiet Massachusetts clergyman, are thus apparent. Far distant be the day when the county of Washington, the State of Ohio, and the whole North-west shall cease to cherish the names and memory of Rufus Putnam and Manasseh Cutler.[1]

The contract for the sale of 1,500,000 acres to the Ohio Company was duly signed Oct. 27, 1787, by Samuel Osgood and Arthur Lee, of the Board of Treasury of the United States, and by Manasseh Cutler and Winthrop Sargent for the Ohio Company. Payment was to be made " in specie, loan office certificates reduced to specie, or certificates of the liquidated debt of the United States." The price was one dollar an acre, liable to a reduction " by an allowance for bad land, and all incidental charges and circumstances whatever; *provided* that all such allowance shall not exceed, in the whole, one-third of a dollar per acre." Rights for bounties of land to the army might be used in payment, but not for more than one-seventh of the whole tract.

The tract was bounded on the east by the seventh range of townships, south by the Ohio, west by the west boundary of the seventeenth range, extending so far north that an east and west line would embrace the number of acres, besides the reservations. These were section sixteen for schools; twenty-nine for the support of religion; eight, eleven and twenty-six to be disposed of by Congress; and two townships for a university.

---

1. In the " Lives of the Early Settlers of Ohio," by Dr. S. P. Hildreth, 107 pages are devoted to General Putnam. A biography of Doctor Cutler is in preparation by Rev. Edwin M. Stone, of Providence, Rhode Island, and will soon be published.

The contract authorized the settlers to enter at once upon half of the tract extending west to the west line of the fifteenth township.

The Company paid half the purchase money when the contract was made; the land to be conveyed when the payment should be complete. But the failure of some of the shareholders to make their payments, the expenses of the Indian war, and losses sustained through their treasurer, so embarrassed the Company that it was impossible for them to pay the remaining $500,000. Early in 1792 the directors met in Philadelphia and memorialized Congress for relief. The Committee of the House of Representatives, to whom the memorial was referred, reported in favor of releasing the Company from the remaining payment, and giving a deed for the whole tract. The House, however, modified this and passed a bill, authorizing a conveyance for that half of the tract already paid for (750,000 acres), another conveyance for 214,285 acres (one-seventh of the original purchase) to be paid for within six months by warrants issued for bounty rights, and one for 100,000 acres which was to be conveyed in tracts of 100 acres as a bounty to each male person of eighteen years of age, being an actual settler. The bill further provided that the Company might receive a conveyance for the remainder of the 1,500,000 acres on the payment for the same within six years at the rate of twenty-five cents an acre with interest. This last provision was stricken out in the Senate, and the one providing for 100,000 acres of donation lands was saved by the casting vote of the Vice-President.

The bill was approved April 21st, and on the 10th of May the three patents were issued to **Rufus Putnam,**

Manasseh Cutler, Robert Oliver, and Griffin Greene, in trust for the Ohio Company of Associates; they were signed by George Washington, President, and Thomas Jefferson, Secretary of State. The three patents for 913,883 acres, (750,000 besides the reservations), for 214,285, and 100,000, bear date the same day, May 10th, 1792. With the exception of one to the State of Pennsylvania, March 3d, 1792, these are the first land patents issued by our government.[1]

The first party of emigrants left Danvers, Massachusetts, Dec. 1st, 1787, conducted by Major Haffield White. The second left Hartford, Connecticut, Jan. 1st, 1788, under Colonel Ebenezer Sproat, General Putnam overtaking them Jan. 24th. The first party reached the Youghiogheny, Jan. 23d, the second Feb. 14th. There they built boats, in which they embarked, April 1st, reaching the mouth of the Muskingum, April 7th. Forty-eight men landed here on that day, and thus began the settlement of the town of Marietta, the county of Washington, the State of Ohio. During that year there came in all one hundred and thirty-two men. There were fifteen families, among them General Tupper's, Major Cushing's, Major Goodale's, and Major Coburn's. At the close of that year, says General Putnam, there was not a single white family within the present State of Ohio save what belonged to the Ohio Company, for Colonel Harmar and most of his officers were proprietors.

In 1762 some Moravian missionaries had gathered a few Indians into a settlement on the Tuscarawas, but it had been broken up by the massacre of the Indians

---

1. These three patents as well as the original contract of October 2, 1787, are in the library of Marietta College.

Marietta in 1788.

in 1782. A fort had been built in 1786 by Major John Doughty on the west bank of the Muskingum, and named for Colonel Josiah Harmar, the commander of the regiment. Fort Laurens had been built by General McIntosh in 1778, but it was abandoned the next year. In 1787, Mr. Isaac Williams had settled in Virginia opposite the mouth of the Muskingum, and the place still bears his name.

This was the situation when General Putnam and his pioneers landed in 1788. And at the close of the year there was no white population in what is now Ohio except that which was here at the mouth of the Muskingum. Yet this little community had distinguished men among them, and was marked by a high degree of intelligence and culture.

Here was General Arthur St. Clair, the governor of the Territory, who was President of Congress when he received his appointment. Here was General Samuel H. Parsons, a distinguished officer of the Revolution and an eminent lawyer and statesman; here also was General James M. Varnum, an officer of distinction, an eloquent lawyer, and a member of the Continental Congress. Both these were judges of the new Territory. These were all men of liberal education, as were Major Winthrop Sargent, secretary of the Territory, Paul Fearing, Return Jonathan Meigs, Jr., Dudley Woodbridge, and various others.

Governor St. Clair was the only governor of the Territory. Winthrop Sargent, the secretary, was appointed governor of Mississippi Territory in 1798, and William Henry Harrison succeeded him as secretary: When Harrison was elected a delegate to Congress in 1799, Charles W. Byrd became secretary.

John Cleves Symmes was one of the three judges of the Territory. He had been a member of Congress, and at the time of his appointment was Chief Justice of the State of New Jersey. He remained in office till Ohio became a State. Judges Parsons and Varnum both died in 1789, and George Turner and Rufus Putnam were appointed in their stead. When Judge Putnam was appointed Surveyor-General of the United States in 1796, he was succeeded by Joseph Gilman; and R. J. Meigs, Jr., was appointed in place of Judge Turner in 1798. Five of the seven judges were citizens of Marietta—Messrs. Parsons, Varnum, Putnam, Gilman and Meigs.

The first Territorial legislature met in 1799, Paul Fearing and Colonel R. J. Meigs being the representatives from this county.[1] Colonel Robert Oliver, a citizen of this county was one of the five members of the Council, or upper house of the legislature, appointed by the President. He continued to be a member of the Council till the State was admitted into the Union in 1803, and for most of the time was the presiding officer of the body. In the second Territorial legislature this county was represented by Ephraim Cutler and William R. Putnam; and the same two gentlemen were re-elected in October, 1802, for the third legislature. Paul Fearing was the delegate to Congress from the Territory from March 1801 to March 1803. In the Convention to frame a State constitution which met at Chillicothe in November, 1802, Washington county was represented by Rufus Putnam, Ephraim Cutler, Benjamin Ives Gilman, and John McIntire. All these

---

1. Colonel R. J. Meigs is often confounded with his son of the same name, who afterward became Governor of Ohio, U. S. Senator, and Postmaster-General.

Washington County Established.

were from Marietta except Mr. McIntire, who lived at Zanesville, then a part of this county.

Governor St. Clair reached Fort Harmar, July 9th, 1788, and was formally received at Marietta on the 15th, General Putnam making an address of welcome. The commissions of the Governor, Judges, and Secretary were read, and thus these officers of the new Territory were inducted into office.

One of the first acts of the Governor was to establish the county of Washington, which was done by proclamation on the 26th of July,[1] with these boundaries:

"Beginning on the bank of the Ohio river where the western boundary line of Pennsylvania crosses it, and running with that line to Lake Erie; thence along the southern shore of said lake to the mouth of Cuyahoga river; thence up said river to the portage between that and the Tuscarawas branch of the Muskingum; thence adown the branch to the forks, at the crossing place above Fort Laurens; thence with a line to be drawn westerly to the portage of that branch of the Big Miami, on which the fort stood that was taken by the French in 1752, until it meets the road from the lower Shawanese town to the Sandusky; thence south to the Scioto river, down that to its mouth, and thence up the Ohio river to the place of beginning." The irregular line from Lake Erie to the Scioto was the boundary between the United States and the Wyandot and Delaware nations, made by the treaty at Fort McIntosh, Jan. 21, 1785.

The county included nearly half of the present State. The next county formed was Hamilton, January 2d,

---

[1]. The volume of the Ohio Statutes, printed in 1807, gives July 27th, as the date, and the same is found in the volume of Land Laws, printed in 1825, in Chase's Statutes, and in the Ohio Statistics for 1876 prepared by the Secretary of State. But an examination of the papers in the State Department at Washington shows that the 26th is the correct date.

1790. Later were established, in what is now Ohio, Adams, July 10th, 1797; Jefferson, July 29th, 1797; Ross, August 20th, 1798; Trumbull, (all of the Western Reserve) July 10th, 1800; Clermont, December 6th, 1800; Fairfield, December 9th, 1800; Belmont, September 7th, 1801.

These nine were the counties when Ohio became a State in 1803. At the first session of the State legislature in March, 1803, eight new counties were made, viz: Scioto, Warren, Butler, Montgomery, Greene, Columbiana, Gallia, and Franklin. The dates of others near us are, Muskingum, 1804; Athens, 1805; Guernsey, 1810; Monroe, 1813; Jackson, 1816; Morgan, Perry and Hocking, 1818; Meigs, 1819; Vinton, 1850; Noble, 1851.

Immediately after the landing on the 7th of April, General Putnam, the Superintendent of the Company, commenced the survey of the town and the eight-acre lots. He also gave his attention to the subject of defense against the Indians. He says: "Besides the propriety of always guarding against savages, I had reason to be cautious, for from consulting the several treaties which had been made with the Indians by our Commissioners (copies of which I had obtained at the War Office as I came on) and other circumstances, I was fully persuaded that the Indians would not be peaceable very long; hence the propriety of immediately erecting a cover for the emigrants who were soon expected. Therefore the hands not necessary to attend the surveys, were set to work in clearing the ground which I had fixed on for erecting the proposed works of defense."

The stockade thus built was called Campus Martius, and was situated about thirty rods from the Muskingum on the north side of what is now Washington

Street. It was one hundred and eighty feet square, with a block-house at each angle, and contained dwelling-houses sufficient for forty or fifty families. In one of these block-houses the first court was held Sept. 2d, 1788, and the same place was used for public worship. After the breaking out of the Indian war in Jan. 1791, a stockade was built at the Point, another at Belpre, and still another at Waterford. That at Belpre was called "Farmers' Castle," and was on the bank of the river opposite the centre of Backus's (now known as Blennerhassett's) island. The one at Waterford, known as "Fort Frye," was on the east bank of the Muskingum, a short distance below the town of Beverly. Some minor fortifications were subsequently erected at Belpre. These various garrisons, with Campus Martius and Fort Harmar, furnished such protection that the settlers passed through the four years of the Indian war with very little loss of life. There was necessarily much hardship and privation, but the pioneers were resolute and intelligent, fertile to contrive and energetic to execute.

The next settlement after Marietta was at Belpre, early in 1789, and another was made at Waterford the same year. This latter was called Plainfield by the people at first, but soon changed to Waterford. In Dec. 1790, Marietta, Belpre and Waterford were organized as townships by the Court of Quarter Sessions. At the March session of the Court in 1797, the county was divided into townships, with the following boundaries:

"*Marietta*, from the seventh range to the western boundary of the ninth range, and bounded north by the donation tract, extending south to include township No. 2, in the ninth range.

Adams, all north of Marietta.

Waterford, all in the county west of Adams and Marietta.

Gallipolis, from the bank of the Ohio on the line between the third and fourth townships of the eleventh range to the west line of the county, thence southerly to the Ohio, and up the Ohio to the place of beginning.

Belpre, all south of Waterford and Marietta, and north of Gallipolis."

The part adjoining Pennsylvania was called *Warren*, and west of that was *Middletown*, both running to the north line of the county.

In the summer of 1797 Jefferson county was formed, taking off these two townships, Warren and Middletown.

In June of that year the people on Duck Creek petitioned for a separate township, and *Salem* was established at the December term of the court. It was bounded on the east by the west line of the seventh range, and on the south by the south line of the donation tract, was five miles wide, and extended to the north line of the county.

In December, 1798, *Newport* was established, and another *Middletown*, embracing a large region around Athens; also *Newtown*, formed from the north part of Waterford, and described as bounded east by Adams, south by Waterford, and north and west by the county lines.

In June, 1800, when the census was taken, there were nine townships in the county, three of which, Gallipolis, Newtown and Middletown, were outside of the present county; leaving Marietta, Belpre, Waterford, Adams, Salem and Newport.

Many changes in the townships have taken place since that time, the present number being twenty-three. A list is given of the whole number that have been created, with the dates of their establishment. Two of the twenty-five — Roxbury and Jolly — have ceased to exist.

Marietta, Belpre, and Waterford, established in 1790; Adams and Salem, 1797; Newport, 1798; Grandview, 1802; Watertown[1] and Roxbury,[2] 1806; Fearing, 1808; Wesley and Warren, 1810; Union,[3] 1812; Lawrence, 1815; Aurelius and Barlow, 1818; Ludlow, 1819; Decatur, 1820; Liberty, 1832; Jolly[4] and Independence, 1840; Fairfield and Palmer, 1851; Dunham, 1856; Muskingum, 1861.

The population in 1870 was 40,609; in 1860, 36,268; in 1850, 29,540. Seven counties exceed it in population by the last census, viz: Cuyahoga, Franklin, Hamilton, Lucas, Montgomery, Muskingum, and Stark.

In 1850, eighteen counties were in advance of Washington. Of the seven counties now in advance of it, all have large cities but two; and of these two, Muskingum has one city of more than 10,000 inhabitants, and Stark has two towns larger than Marietta, and one of about the same size. We may say, then, that no agricultural county in the State has a larger population than Washington. The counties exceeding it in 1850 and behind it in 1870 are Belmont, Butler, Clermont, Columbiana, Fairfield, Guernsey, Licking, Richland, Ross, Trumbull, Tuscarawas and Wayne. In the twenty years only one county has outstripped it—Lucas, which contains the thriving city, Toledo.

1. Watertown was called Wooster till 1824.
2. A part of Roxbury was annexed to Morgan county in 1851, and the rest merged in the new township of Palmer.
3. Union has now (1877) been divided between Adams, Muskingum, Warren and Watertown.
4. A part of Jolly was annexed to Monroe county in 1851, and the rest to Grandview in 1859.

From 1850 to 1870 fourteen counties in Ohio retrograded in population, and twelve of these did the same from 1860 to 1870.

Since 1850 the population of Washington has suffered some reduction by the formation of Noble county, and by the annexation of a part of the township of Roxbury to Morgan county, and of parts of Liberty, Ludlow and Jolly to Monroe county.

It should be noted that the tendency of the population in the United States is toward the cities in an increasing ratio. Calling those places cities which have a population of 8,000, the census shows that in 1790 the cities had one-thirtieth of the whole population; in 1820, one-twentieth; in 1850, one-eighth; in 1870, one-fifth. This makes the growth of this county more noteworthy.

The movement of the center of population of the United States has been westward about fifty miles a decade, and along a parallel of latitude nearly coincident with the south line of this county. In 1790 the center was a little east of Baltimore, in latitude 39° 16'; in 1870 it was fifty miles easterly from Cincinnati, in latitude 39° 12'. In the eighty years it has not deviated more than one-sixth of a degree from its general line of movement westward.

The area of Washington county is about 613 square miles, which is thirty-five per cent. above the average of the counties. The density of population is almost exactly that of the State as a whole, being a fraction above sixty-six to the square mile. A removal of the county-seat to Waterford was suggested in 1817, but the formation of Morgan county the next winter quieted whatever agitation there was.

Formation of the State.

The ordinance of 1787 provided for the formation of not less than three nor more than five states from the North-west Territory, and the boundaries were given. When any division should have 60,000 inhabitants, it might form a state constitution. The territory of Indiana was formed in 1800, and the census of that year showed a population of 42,000 in the eastern division. After the adjournment of the legislature in January, 1802, another census gave 45,028 inhabitants, and an effort was made to secure the admission of Ohio into the Union. In modern times the people of a territory are usually anxious to exchange the territorial for the state government at the earliest day, and most of our new states have been admitted with a population insufficient for a single representative. But the people of Washington county were in no such haste. Almost unanimously they were opposed to the formation of a state when Congress passed the enabling act in April, 1802.

In June, 1801, a convention of delegates from most of the towns of the county was held, at which it was unanimously resolved; "That in our opinion, it would be highly impolitic, and very injurious to the inhabitants of this territory, to enter into a state government at this time." Among the delegates were Paul Fearing, Elijah Backus, Isaac Pierce, Silas Bent, Robert Oliver, Gilbert Devol, Joseph Barker and others.

In December of the same year the territorial legislature requested Congress to change the western boundary of the eastern division from the Miami river to the Scioto. As such a change would diminish the population as well as the area, its effect would be to postpone the time of admission. The people of this county were in favor of the alteration, and both their representatives voted for it. But Congress did not consent to the change in boundary, and favored the formation of a state, although the population was only about two-thirds of the number contemplated by the ordinance.

The advocates and opponents of the formation of a state were strong in the expression of their opinions, and prove that party feeling had existence before our day. Thomas Worthington, afterwards Governor of Ohio, in a letter to Col. R. J. Meigs, speaks of the endeavors "to curb a tyrant," referring to Governor St. Clair; and in another he speaks of "the uncommon pains taken by Arthur the First to show that our treasury is in debt." But he does not regard the change from territory to state as in itself desirable; "I am by no means an advocate for a state government if we can by any means have tolerable harmony under the present. There are a number of reasons against going into a state government, it is true, but can any situation be more disagreeable than the past has been and the present is." General Joseph Darlinton, a member of the first territorial legislature from Adams county, writes to Mr. Fearing in March, 1802, that he thinks the people of his county are unanimous for admission into the Union, " and congratulate themselves on the prospect of having it soon in their power to shake off the iron fetters of aristocracy, and in the downfall of the tory party in this territory," and hope for the day when they shall be "free from the control of an arbitrary chief."

On the other hand, Judge Woodbridge writes to Mr. Fearing in January and March 1802, alluding to the foolish talk about "aristocrats" and "tories," and expressing his opinion that scarcely a citizen of the county

Formation of the State.

would wish to come into a state government. Mr. Benjamin Ives Gilman writes warmly, and intimates that those who wished to be in favor with the national administration were advocates of the change. He is "disgusted with politics," and is very severe on the President for the change in postmaster at Marietta. "It is the most pitiful measure that ever was taken, and reflects disgrace on all concerned in the removal." Hon. Solomon Sibley, formerly of Marietta, but then of Detroit, writes to Judge Burnet in 1802, "I did expect that Congress would not readily have interfered in the petty political squabbles of the territory." "We may thank our good friends Judges S. and M., and *Sir Thomas* for what is done." The allusion is here to the exclusion by Congress of the eastern part of Michigan from the eastern district of the territory, to which it properly belonged.

But Congress by an act passed April 30th, 1802, authorized a convention to form a constitution. The delegates were elected October 12th, and the convention met November 1st. Business of this character was transacted with promptness in those days; for the constitution was completed and the convention had adjourned before the close of the month. The constitution thus formed was not submitted to the people for ratification, which is the more remarkable as the convention itself was called by Congress without any request on the part of the legislature, and without the opinion of the inhabitants being taken. The question on submitting the constitution to the people was taken in the convention and lost by a vote of 27 to 7. Those who voted in favor of submitting the constitution to the people

---

1. Judge Sibley married the daughter of Colonel Ebenezer Sproat, and grand-daughter of Commodore Abraham Whipple. He was a member of the legislative Council of the Territory.

were Messrs. Cutler, Gilman, McIntire and Putnam, of this county, Bezaleel Wells and Nathan Updegraff of Jefferson county, and John Reily of Hamilton. It may be stated that Judge Cutler also cast his vote in the negative, though solitary and alone, on the question of forming a constitution at that time.

The convention adjourned on the 29th of November and copies of the constitution were forwarded to Congress by Edward Tiffin, president of the convention whose letter is dated "Chillicothe, N. W. Territory, Dec. 4, 1802." On the 7th of January, 1803, the Senate appointed a committee to "inquire whether any, and if any, what legislative measures may be necessary for admitting the State of Ohio into the Union, and extending to that State the laws of the United States." This committee reported on the 19th that the constitution and state government was republican and in uniformity with the principles of the ordinance of 1787, and that it was necessary to establish a District Court within the State to carry into complete effect the laws of the United States. Such a bill was reported on the 27th of January, passed the Senate February 7th, passed the House of Representatives February 12th, and was approved by the President, February 19th.

As the constitution of the United States gives to Congress alone the power to admit new states, and as the act of February 19th, was the first recognition of Ohio by Congress, it seems clear that the proper date of the admission of Ohio into the Union is February 19, 1803.[1]

---

[1] Various other dates for the admission of Ohio have been given, as April 30th, June 30th, and November 29th, 1802; March 1st, and March 3d, 1803. That of November 29th, 1802, is the one most frequently met with. It is the date of the adjournment of the convention which framed the constitution. If the act of a convention could change a territory into a state in the case of Ohio, why not in the case of Indiana or Colorado?

The constitution provided that an election of governor, members of the assembly, sheriffs and coroners should take place on the second Tuesday of January, and that the legislature should meet on the first Tuesday of March. Edward Tiffin, president of the constitutional convention, was elected the first governor, and was inaugurated March 3d, the legislature having commenced its session March 1st.

As Washington was the first county established in the North-west Territory, so Marietta was the first town incorporated. As a township it was established by the Court of Quarter Sessions in 1790; as a town it was incorporated by the territorial legislature December 2d, 1800. The town of Athens was incorporated December 6th, of the same year, Cincinnati January 1st, 1802, and Chillicothe, January 4th, 1802.

The act of incorporation of Marietta was amended in 1812; in 1825 a charter was obtained, and another in 1835. The town, as incorporated in 1800, seems to have been identical in boundary with the township, extending north to the donation tract, and being twelve miles east and west. The charter of 1825 erected into a town corporate such parts of the old town as were contained in "the town plat, recorded in the Recorder's office." This act divided the town into three wards: the second ward embracing the part west of the Muskingum, and the first and third lying respectively south and north of "Stone Bridge Creek." The act of 1835 gave the same division into wards, but "Stone Bridge Creek" is called "Market Square Run." The same stream in the the days of the early settlers bore the name of "Tyber Creek."

By the act of incorporation of 1800 the town officers were to be elected in town meeting by ballot, and votes on other subjects were to be taken by holding up the hand. Besides the chairman of the town meeting, the voters were to elect by a majority vote a town clerk, a town treasurer, and " three or five able and discreet persons of good moral character, to be styled the town council."

There was no Mayor till 1825. By the act of that year each ward could elect three trustees, and these nine could elect from their own number a mayor, recorder, and treasurer, who with the other six should constitute the town council. The act of 1835 made the mayor to be elected by the people; he was to preside in the town council, but have no vote. The act itself was not to take effect unless accepted by a vote of the people. In 1837 Harmar was incorporated as a separate town, and Marietta had but two wards from that time till 1854. In October, 1853, Marietta became a city of the second class, in accordance with the general law of May 3d, 1852. In the election of 1854 the council was elected from three wards; the first being below Butler Street, the second and third above Butler, one west, and the other east, of Fourth.

In the matter of local government there are two very different systems in the United States. In New England the *town*—answering to the "township" of Ohio—is the political unit. In all the Southern States till recently, and in most of them now, the *county* is clothed with the chief political power. The town has no existence, or, if existing, it is devoid of all political significance.

The divisions subordinate to the county are generally called *precincts* in the South. In Mississippi

The System of Local Government in Ohio.

whole counties have no other names for their subdivisions than those furnished by the ranges and townships; as if we should know Lawrence only as Township 3, Range 7. In North Carolina the county seems to be divided numerically; as if Belpre were merely No. 4.

The Ohio system is not strictly the town system of New England, or the county system of the South. It is what is called the " compromise " system in the census report for 1870, and is found in the great Middle States and in most of the Western. The political power is divided between the county and the town; the former has much more importance than in New England, and the latter has less.

In the incorporation of Marietta as a town in 1800, the features of the town system are seen. The establishment of the Court of Quarter Sessions with many of the powers now exercised by the county commissioners, showed the influence of the other system. General Putnam and his associates from New England were able to incorporate into the new communities of the West some of the features of the town system, while Governor St. Clair from Pennsylvania and John Cleves Symmes from New Jersey introduced various laws from those states. We may be thankful that we have as much as we have of the town system. The opinion of Mr. Jefferson on the merits of this system, Virginian though he was, was strongly expressed at different times. He recommended the division of the counties of Virginia into wards of six miles square. " These wards, called townships in New England, are the vital principle of their governments, and have proved themselves the wisest invention ever devised by the wit of man for the perfect exercise of self-government and for its preservation." Again he says: "These little republics would be the main strength of the great one. We owe to them the vigor given to our revolution in its commencement in the Eastern States, and by them the Eastern States were enabled to repeal the embargo in opposition to the Middle, Southern and Western States and their large and lubberly divisions into counties which can never be assembled."

The first court held in the territory was that of the Court of Common Pleas at Campus Martius, September 2d, 1788. A procession was formed at the Point, where most of the settlers resided, in the following order: The high sheriff, with his drawn sword; the citizens; the officers of the garrison at Fort Harmar; the members of the bar; the supreme judges; the governor and clergyman; and the newly appointed judges of the court, Generals Rufus Putnam and Benjamin Tupper. Rev. Dr. Manasseh Cutler, one of the directors of the Ohio Company, then here on a visit, opened the court with prayer; and Colonel Ebenezer Sproat, the sheriff, made official proclamation that "a court is opened for the administration of even-handed justice, to the poor and the rich, to the guilty and the innocent, without respect of persons." General Putnam alluding to this first court says: "happily for the credit of the people there was no suit either civil or criminal brought before the court."

It is probable that the court continued to be held in the north-west block-house of Campus Martius for a number of years. As early as 1792 the Court of Quarter Sessions submitted estimates for a court-house and jail—$1,000 for each. In 1793 Thomas Lord was directed to take a log-house near Campus Martius and

The Court-House of 1800.

fit it up for a jail. Among the old papers in one of Dr. Hildreth's collections of manuscripts, now in the college library, is a bill of Nathan McIntosh for two thousand and four hundred brick "delivered for the use of the old court-house," bearing date December, 1797. This refers to a block-house at the Point, used then for courts.

In 1799, Griffin Greene and Timothy Buell were appointed, by the Court of Common Pleas, commissioners to build a jail and court-house. They estimated the cost to be $3001,81. Contracts were made with Joshua Wells to frame and raise the building; with Joshua Shipman to weather-board and shingle the house, make the doors, lay the floors, etc.; with James Lawton to do the mason work; and with Gilbert Devol, Jr., to furnish "three thousand weight of good iron" manufactured into spikes, bolts, grates, etc., etc., for which he was to receive sixteen cents a pound. The building was completed in 1800. The court-room was in the second story, being forty feet long by twenty broad. The walls of the jail were three feet thick, and the whole was built in the most substantial manner. Dr. Hildreth speaks of it in 1842 as at that time "one of the strongest prisons in the state."

The subject of a new court-house was agitated in 1819. At a meeting of citizens held September 13th, a committee, consisting of Governor R. J. Meigs, Hon. Levi Barber, and D. H. Buell, Esq., reported in favor of a new building to be located at the corner of Second and Putnam streets—the present site. The next day the county commissioners passed a resolution to the same effect. The matter appeared to rest for two years, when the commissioners appointed Joseph Holden, the county treasurer, to superintend the delivery of the materials. In November, 1821, they advertised for a *plan*, the building to be forty-eight feet square, with a fire-proof office sixteen feet square in each corner.

In the winter and spring of 1822, there was no little excitement as to the site of the new court-house. Many were opposed to the corner of Second and Putnam as too low, and favored a higher location. Some advocated the elevated square on Washington street; others wanted it on Fifth street near the mound. Petitions and counter-petitions were sent to the commissioners. On the 6th of March they decided to locate it on Fifth street, south of the cemetery, provided a better subscription could be obtained than for any other location. Three weeks later a public meeting was held, and a majority voted for the "Thierry lots"—where Judge Ewart now resides. At a meeting in April, the commissioners resolved upon that location; but in the same month they re-considered their action, and again and finally, decided in favor of the corner of Second and Putnam streets. The edifice was completed in 1823.

In 1854, the additional building on the north was erected, in which is the office of the probate judge. The court-house of 1823 has undergone another transformation the present year by adding to its length and height. The present jail was built in 1848, according to a plan furnished by Hon. R. E. Harte. It was proposed to place it on the same lot with the court-house, but in consideration of $500, paid by Dr. S. P. Hildreth and Mrs. Martha B. Wilson, living on the adjoining lots, the commissioners agreed to erect it upon the old site. It should be stated that the land where the present jail is, and where the old court-house stood, was given to the county by Judge Dudley Woodbridge; and that on

Punishment in Early Times.

which the present court-house stands was given by Col. Ebenezer Sproat. The bell is the same that was on the old court-house. It bears the inscription, "Barzillai Davison, Norwich, 1802."

In the early days the jail served a double purpose: it was "for the reception and confinement of debtors and criminals." There were, however, two separate apartments for the two classes of prisoners. But criminals were punished in other ways besides confinement. By the law of September 6th, 1788, whipping and putting in the pillory and stocks, are enumerated among the modes of punishment. Thirty-nine "stripes" was the maximum. But by a state law of 1805, fifty-nine stripes might be inflicted for robbery, and one hundred for a second offence. In 1811, fifty stripes might be inflicted for destroying fruit trees. In 1788, drunkenness was punished by fine, but in failure of payment the offender was to sit in "the stocks for the space of one hour."

In 1800, Robert Oliver, Griffin Greene and Robert Safford, a committee appointed for the purpose, reported "that the north-west corner of the lot donated to the county by Col. E. Sproat is the most convenient place for the pound, and that in the same lot is sufficient space for the pillory, stocks and whipping post." The report is accompanied with drawings, made by Mr. Greene, who also drew the plan of the old court-house. The whipping-post, pillory and stocks, thus erected on the lot where the court-house now stands, remained probably till after 1820.

In this connection it may be stated that in 1856 the county commissioners of this county, in accordance with a law of the State, made provision for the labor on roads, quarries, etc., of convicts confined in the county jail, thus relieving the county in part of the cost of their maintenance.

Provision for aiding the poor was made as early as 1790, it having been made the duty of the Court of Quarter Sessions to appoint overseers of the poor in each township. In 1795, a very elaborate act, of thirty-two sections, was adopted from the statutes of Pennsylvania. "Two substantial inhabitants of every township" were to be appointed yearly as overseers. The law contains this singular provision, that the overseers going out of office should return to the justices the names of two or more substantial inhabitants, from which number their successors should be appointed for the ensuing year. And a failure to make such return made the person liable in the sum of twenty-five dollars.

By a law of the first territorial assembly it was made the duty of the overseers to cause all the poor each year " to be farmed out at public vendue, or outcry," to the lowest bidder.

From 1804 the overseers of the poor were elected in each township.

County poor-houses were authorized in 1816, to be built under the direction of the county commissioners, who were also to appoint the directors. The term of service of the directors was at first seven years, but was reduced to three. The town of Marietta applied to the commissioners in 1819 to build a poor-house for the county, but the application was rejected because, as was alleged, the townships would prefer to support their own poor. No step was taken in this direction till 1835, when land was bought of Dr. Jonas Moore for $1,200, and a contract was made with Daniels, Westgate and Alcock to erect a house for $2,040.

The Children's Home.

In June, 1836, the commissioners appointed Sampson Cole, Eben Gates, and Wyllys Hall directors. In March, 1838, petitions were presented to change the location, and in December of that year a farm of 198 acres was purchased for $2,536.58—the present location. The next spring the other house and farm was sold to Dr. E. B. Perkins for $4,000.

Since 1842 the directors have been elected by the people, and in 1850 the legislature changed[1] the name "County Poorhouse" to "County Infirmary."

The Children's Home has been in successful operation for nearly ten years. The one in this county was the first established under the act providing for institutions of this character. The idea itself, indeed, originated here. About 1858 Miss Catherine Fay, now Mrs. Ewing, took into her house a number of poor children, for whom she furnished support and instruction, with some aid from the benevolent and some allowance from the infirmary directors. A bill was subsequently introduced into the legislature by Hon. W. F. Curtis, the senator from this district, authorizing county commissioners to establish Children's Homes and provide for their support by taxation. The act was passed in May, 1866, Hon. S. S. Knowles then being the senator. The history of the institution, which was established soon after the passage of the act, is familiar to the people of the county. The present trustees are Hon. William R. Putnam, Hon. F. A. Wheeler, and Mr. W. Dudley Devol. Judge Putnam has taken a deep interest in it from the first, and has devoted to it a great deal of time and attention.[1] Dr. Simeon D. Hart is the superintendent, and Mrs. Hart the matron.

The first sermon in the Territory was preached Sun-

---

1. For changes see Appendix.

day, July 10th, 1788, in the hall of the north-west blockhouse in Campus Martius by Rev. William Breck. Rev. Dr. Manasseh Cutler, who visited the colony the first summer, preached a number of times. In the spring of 1789, Rev. Daniel Story came out, having been employed by the Ohio Company. He preached for a number of years, as well at Belpre and Waterford as at Marietta. He received a part of his support from the Company and a part from the people.

The *Congregational* Church at Marietta was organized December 6th, 1796, composed of members residing at Marietta, Belpre, Waterford, and Vienna, Virginia. The first deacons were Dr. Josiah Hart of Marietta, Joseph Spencer of Vienna, Benjamin Miles of Belpre, and Nathan Proctor of Waterford. Rev. Daniel Story was the first pastor, installed by a council convened at Hamilton, Mass., August 15th, 1798. Rev. Samuel P. Robbins became the pastor January 8th, 1806; Rev. Luther G. Bingham, May 3, 1826; Rev. Thomas Wickes, D. D., July 28th, 1840; and the present pastor, Rev. Theron H. Hawks, D. D., October 27th, 1869. The pastorate of Dr. Wickes extended from 1840 to 1869, being longer than any other in the county.

The Congregational Church at Belpre was organized in 1826, and that at Harmar in 1840. The Town Hall in Harmar was used for worship till November 27th, 1847, when the present church edifice was dedicated, having been erected on ground given by the late David Putnam, Esq. There are at this time ten Congregational Churches in the county.

The *First Religious Society* in Marietta was formed March 2d, 1801. The original articles of association, with 128 autograph signatures, have been preserved. This society was incorporated by the legislature February 4th, 1807, two others being incorporated the same winter—an Episcopal society at Worthington, and a Presbyterian at Cincinnati. These were the first religious societies incorporated in the State. This First Society in Marietta was connected with the Congregational church, and worshiped in the "Muskingum Academy," till the present church was dedicated May 28th, 1809.

A *Presbyterian* congregation was gathered in Marietta very early, and Rev. Stephen Lindley was employed as minister in January, 1804. On the 18th of that month the *Second Religious Society* was formed. The date of the organization of the church I cannot give, or the length of time that Mr. Lindley ministered to them. On the declaration of war with Great Britian in 1812, he became a chaplain in the army. January 25th, 1813, the legislature incorporated the " First Presbyterian Society in the town of Marietta, called the Second Religious Society." This society received aid from the ministerial funds derived from section 29, till 1818.

A Presbyterian church was formed at Waterford at an early day. It is supposed to be the same as the present Cumberland Presbyterian church at Beverly, and is probably the oldest church but one in the county.

A Presbyterian church was organized at Marietta in 1841, which continued in existence about twenty-five years, though regular worship was not maintained during the whole period. The frame edifice on Third street near Greene was erected by them.

The Fourth Street Presbyterian Church was formed in 1865, and their house of worship on Fourth street near Wooster, was erected the same year. Both this and the one formed in 1841 were chiefly colonies from the Congregational church. There are now six Presbyterian churches in the county.

Besides the "First" and the "Second" Religious Societies formed in Marietta in 1801 and 1804, there were three other societies organized in 1805 and 1806.

The "*Religious Meeting House Society,*" organized April 15th, 1805, seems not to have contemplated the support of public worship, but simply "the important and laudable purpose of erecting a Meeting House in the town of Marietta, to be consecrated and devoted to the public worship of Almighty God." To this end the members "solemnly and irrevocably transfer" all their dividends from the ministerial rents for the period of seven years. It was this society that commenced the erection of the large brick building on Third street below Greene. As some of those who were active in this society were among those who in 1804 employed Rev. Mr. Lindley, it may be inferred that this edifice was ultimately intended as the place of worship for the Presbyterian church. But the building was never completed as a church. Both the "Second Religious Society" and the "Religious Meeting House Society" continued for some years to receive dividends from the rents of section 29; the former to 1818, and the latter to 1816.

The "*Fourth Religious Society*" was formed in 1805, and was composed of persons living east of Duck Creek. The last ministerial dividend to that society was in 1812.

The "*Union Religious Society*" was formed in 1805 or 1806, and its members were chiefly or wholly made up of residents of Harmar. It received dividends from the ministerial rents to 1818.

It will be noted that of the five religious societies organized in Marietta from 1801 to 1806, no one had a denominational designation, and that only one of the five is still in existence. The other four had become extinct before 1820.

The first *Methodist Episcopal* organization in Marietta was in 1812. The first house of worship was built in 1814—the frame edifice on Second street north of Scammel, now occupied by the German Methodists. The church on Putnam street was built in 1839, and hence its name, The Centenary Church. The Methodist church in Harmar, now called Crawford Chapel, was formed in 1849, and the second charge in Marietta, or Whitney Chapel, in 1860.[1.]

The *Universalist* Society was formed in 1817, and the frame building on Second street, formerly used for worship, was built about 1842. For some years the members of this society have worshiped with the Unitarians, but they still maintain their distinctive organization. An act was passed February 2d, 1832, to incorporate the "First Universalian Religious Library Society of Marietta." Mr. John Delafield, Jr., in his pamphlet published in 1834, says, the "society devotes the property which annually accrues to its treasury to the acquisition of an extensive and valuable miscellaneous library." This appropriation of their portion of the ministerial funds long since ceased, and the library is not now in existence.

A Universalist society was organized in Harmar in 1839, and continued till 1849. The church in Belpre

---
1. The two congregations in Marietta have now united, and worship in the Centenary Church.

was formed in 1823, and is said to be the oldest *church* of the denomination in the State. The present number of organizations in the county is nine.

A *Baptist* church was organized in 1818 in Marietta township. The first edifice in the county was the brick church near Cornerville, east of the Little Muskingum. The organization in the town of Marietta was in 1833, and the edifice on Church street was built in 1835. The present church on Putnam street was erected in 1854. Rev. Jeremiah Dale was one of the early preachers in this region, doing missionary work over a large territory. He died in 1831. Rev. Hiram Gear, who died in 1843, had been pastor of the church in Marietta for six years. There are at this time fourteen Baptist churches in the county.

A *Protestant Episcopal* organization was made as early as 1827 in Marietta, and an act "to incorporate St. Luke's Church" was passed by the legislature Jan. 9th, 1833. The church building at the corner of Fourth and Scammel streets was opened November 22d, 1834, and occupied by this church till 1857, when the present house on Second street was erected. Rev. Dr. John Boyd has been here since 1850, making his continuous clerical service longer than that of any other clergyman in the county except Rev. Dr. Wickes.

The *Roman Catholic* Society was organized in 1839, and their present church edifice on Fourth street was erected in 1853. There are two churches in Union township and one in Ludlow.

In 1840 the first *German* Church in Marietta was organized — *the German Evangelical Church, St. Paul's.* Though not in organic connection with the Lutheran Synod of Ohio, their present pastor is a mem-

Religious Organizations.

ber of that body. Their house of worship, at the corner of Fifth and Scammel streets, was built in 1848.

The *German Methodist Episcopal Church* was formed in 1842, and has occupied from its organization the house on Second street, built by the Methodist congregation now worshiping at the Centenary church.

In 1851 a third German organization was made, the *German Evangelical Church of St. Lucas*. They occupy as their place of worship the house erected by the Protestant Episcopal church at the corner of Fourth and Scammel streets.

The *Unitarian* Church at the corner of Third and Putnam streets was erected in 1855. This edifice, which is the finest in the place, was built at the expense of Mr. Nahum Ward, and with organ and bell was presented to the society.

The Church of the *United Brethren* was organized in 1857, and their house on Fourth street north of Greene was erected in 1866.

In 1871 the *African Methodist* Church first received aid from the ministerial rents, though they had maintained worship for some time before that. For some years they have occupied the frame building on Third street built for a Presbyterian church.

In 1812 a Bible Society was formed at Marietta, of which General Rufus Putnam was president. It is referred to by the correspondents of General Putnam as the "Ohio Bible Society," and bibles and testaments were sent here from New York and Philadelphia, to be distributed at prominent points both in this State and in Indiana Territory.

In 1814 (October 10th), was formed the "Society for the promotion of good morals." The object was "to promote good morals, and discountenance vice universally; particularly to discourage profaneness, gross breaches of the Sabbath, idleness, and intemperance; and especially to discourage intemperance." The first officers were Rev. S. P. Robbins, president, David I. Burr, vice president, and David Putnam, secretary.

In the fall of 1818 a committee, consisting of David Putnam, Wm. R. Putnam, and James Whitney, wrote to Governor Worthington asking him to call the attention of the legislature to the subject of intemperance, which he did. They then memorialized the legislature on the subject asking for action, and saying, "It has been a subject of regret to your memorialists while perusing the statutes of this State, that no paragraph or expression can be found which censures this offence."

In 1817 this society voted to establish a Sunday School, and the records for 1819 show that three schools were in operation under its general care. One was at the "Muskingum Academy," under the charge of Mr. William Holyoke, one at the "brick house on Point Harmar," under Mr. William Slocomb, and one for small scholars at "Buell's school room" at the Point, under the care of Mrs. Whipple and Mrs. Merwin.

A temperance society was formed July 31, 1830. The officers were, president, Ephraim Emerson; vice presidents, Rev. Jacob Young and Robert Crawford; secretary, Rev. L. G. Bingham; treasurer, Wyllys Hall; executive committee, Caleb Emerson, Junia Jennings, Douglas Putnam, Samuel Shipman.

From the character of the early settlers more attention to education might have been expected than in most new settlements. As early as 1790 the directors of the Ohio Company appropriated money for schools in Marietta, Belpre and Waterford. From the very first there were schools in which instruction was given by persons of high literary attainments. At Belpre, Daniel Mayo, a graduate of Harvard, taught for a number of winters, and others who had received collegiate training were employed to some extent in the work of instruction.

Before the first decade had passed steps were taken to establish a regular academy at Marietta. On the 29th of April, 1797, a number of the citizens convened "to consider measures for promoting the education of youth," and a committee was appointed to prepare a plan of a house suitable for the instuction of youth and for religious purposes, to estimate the expense and recommend a site. The committee consisted of General Rufus Putnam, Paul Fearing, Griffin Greene, R. J. Meigs, Jr., Charles Greene, and Joshua Shipman. At the end of a week the committee made their report at an adjourned meeting. They presented a plan of the house, estimated the expense at $1,000, and recommended city lot No. 605—the lot on Front street, north of the Congregational church. As the best mode of raising the money they suggested "that the possessors of ministerial lands lying on the Ohio river between Heart's ditch and the south end of Front street, and on Front street, and between Front street and the Muskingum river, do pay at the rate of one dollar for every one-third of an acre which they respectively possess." Assessments on other lands were recommended and a subscription to meet deficiencies.

The report was accepted as to the plan of the house, the cost and the location; but the method of securing funds was modified so as "to assess the possessors of ministerial lands in proportion to the value of their respective possessions." The sums thus paid, either by assessment or subscription, were to be considered as stock, at the rate of ten dollars a share; and the stockholders were entitled to votes according to their shares. At a meeting in August of that year fifty-nine shares were represented, of which thirty belonged to General Putnam.

Thus originated the Muskingum Academy, which was probably the first structure of the kind erected in the North-west territory. It was used for educational purposes till 1832, when it was removed to Second street, near the Rhodes block, where it is still standing. It was also used on the Sabbath as a place of worship till 1809, when the Congregational church was completed.

David Putnam, Esq., a graduate of Yale College, was the first instructor in the Muskingum Academy. Among the others who taught before the removal of the old academy, were Benjamin F. Stone, Morris B. Belknap, N. K. Clough, Caleb Emerson, Jonas Moore, David Gilmore, Edwin Putnam, Elisha Huntington,[1] William A. Whittlesey, William Slocomb, John K. Joline.

In 1830, Rev. L. G. Bingham established "The Institute of Education," comprising an Infant School, Primary School, Ladies Seminary and High School. The next year Mr. Mansfield French became joint proprietor with Mr. Bingham; Mr. N. Brown, a graduate of Williams College, having charge of the High School, and Miss Spalding, from Ipswich, Mass., of the Ladies Seminary. In 1832 Mr. Henry Smith, a graduate of Middlebury College, was the principal of the High

---

1. Afterwards Lieutenant Governor of Massachusetts.

Marietta College Established.

School, and Miss D. T. Wells—afterwards Mrs. D. P. Bosworth—was associated with Miss Spalding in the Ladies Seminary. The High School prospered greatly, and in the December following a charter was obtained under the style of the "Marietta Collegiate Institute," and a board of trustees was appointed. In the autumn of 1833 it was opened as a public institution in what is now the dormitory building on the College square. A new charter was obtained February 14th, 1835, under the name of "Marietta College."

The Seminary for young ladies also passed into the hands of the same corporation, though the two institutions were kept distinct so far as instruction was concerned. The ladies at the head of it were successively Miss Spalding, Miss Wells, Miss C. M. Webster, Miss S. Jaquith, and Mrs. L. Tenney. In 1843 the seminary property was sold by the trustees, but the institution was continued for a number of years under the charge of Mrs. Tenney.

The original trustees of the college were Luther G. Bingham, John Cotton, Caleb Emerson, John Mills, John Crawford, Arius Nye, Douglas Putnam, Jonas Moore, and Anselm T. Nye. But Messrs. John Crawford and Arius Nye did not act under the second charter. The members of the first faculty were Henry Smith, professor of Languages; D. Howe Allen, professor of Mathematics; Milo P. Jewett, professor of Rhetoric and principal of the Teachers department; and Samuel Maxwell, principal of the Preparatory department. In 1835 Rev. Joel H. Linsley was elected president, and held the office till 1846. President Henry Smith was at the head of the college from 1846, to 1855, when he was succeeded by the present president, Israel W. Andrews.

The first class was graduated in 1838, since which the succession of classes has been unbroken. The whole number of graduates in the classical course is four hundred and thirty-five, with twelve who have completed a scientific course.[1] Of the whole number, one hundred and forty-three, or thirty-two per cent. have been from Washington county. For the last few years the county has furnished to the college classes an average of forty students, being one college student for each thousand of the population.

The pioneers of this settlement and the directors of the Ohio Company showed their interest in education by causing to be inserted in their contract with the government for their purchase, a provision that two townships of land should be appropriated for a university, and one section in each township for schools. The two townships, as General Putnam says in a letter to Hon. Paul Fearing, dated November 20th, 1800, were " in fact more of a donation of the Ohio Company than of the United States, as this was a part of the consideration which induced the directors of the company to agree to purchase the other lands." The good General seemed to be disappointed even at that early day, that the generous example of the company had not been followed. He was looking for gifts to be made by individuals, and writes: " Is there no public spirit to be found in the Territory except only in the proprietors of the Ohio Company ? * * Is it not possible that some worthy, able, public-spirited gentlemen in Adams and Ross counties * * may make donations to the institution ?" He evidently did not expect that the land would make a sufficient endowment, but was looking for the gift of the company to

---

[1]. This includes the class of 1877.

Educational Institutions.

be supplemented by other gifts from generous, public-spirited men.

The author of a recent work on American State Universities, after speaking of the obstacles which the institution at Athens has had to encounter, adds: "The very movers in the work, long ago discouraged, established a college at their beloved Marietta." The college at Marietta may indeed be justly regarded as the child of the pioneers; for by the descendants of those that gave the two townships has it been established and sustained; and its eminent success may be attributed largely to this, that it embodies and represents the spirit and culture of those who came in the last century to found here a new home.

It is an item of historical interest that about sixty of the graduates of the college are the lineal descendants of those who settled on the lands of the Ohio Company prior to 1800, representing more than forty of the early settlers.

As illustrative of the continuance of interest in the institution, and the increase in successive donations as the ability to give increased, this fact may be stated. Among the donors in the first effort made at Marietta in March, 1833, there were seven whose contributions amounted in the aggregate to $2,250; the gifts ranging from $50 to $1,000. The total donations made to the college by these seven gentlemen to the present time amount to over $95,000. And the citizens of Marietta and the immediate vicinity have given, in all, the sum of $165,000.

An institution was opened at Beverly, in November, 1842, under the name of the Beverly College, Rev. J. P. Wethee, president. It was started under the auspices of the Cumberland Presbyterian Church. The building was erected by Mr. John Dodge, and Mr. Benjamin Dana made a donation in land. Besides the building and lot there is a fund of two thousand dollars or more. The institution has been in operation most of the time since 1842, as an academy or high school, and a considerable number of young people of both sexes have enjoyed its advantages; some have been prepared to enter college, in a few instances joining the Sophomore or Junior classes.

An Academy was commenced in Harmar about 1845, through the efforts of some of her citizens, and continued in successful operation for a number of years, till the re-organization of the public schools. As an academy, and as the high school department of the public schools, it was an efficient institution, preparing a large number of young men for college. Among the teachers may be named Messrs. Henry Bates, John Giles, and George H. Howison.

The Marietta public schools up to 1849, were five in number, in five separate districts, each with its own directors. The question of consolidating the schools under one board of education, and introducing the union or graded system, was first agitated in the fall of 1848. At that time but few towns in Ohio had introduced the new system, but its workings had been so successful that the people of Marietta were disposed to make trial of it. The first board of education was elected in the spring of 1849, consisting of E. H. Allen, I. W. Andrews, Lucius Brigham, Robert Crawford, T. W. Ewart, and Rufus E. Harte; and the schools went into operation under what was then known as the Akron law.

Educational Institutions.

The Marietta Liberal Institute was established in 1849, under the patronage of the Universalists. An edifice was erected on Second street below Butler. Instruction in the higher branches was given to young people of both sexes for a number of years, and the institution was well patronized. The first principal was Mr. Paul Kendall.

For some years a school has been in operation in Wesley township, the Bartlett Academy, which is believed to be in a flourishing condition.

Besides Marietta and Harmar, the towns of Belpre, Beverly, and Newport, and perhaps others, have the graded system of public schools in operation. Belpre has just erected a fine building, probably the best public school edifice in the county.

The township of Lawrence happens to be the possessor of an educational fund of some $25,000, derived from an oil well on one of the school district lots; which it is hoped may be used for the support of a central school of higher grade for the more advanced pupils of the township.

As an educational item mention should be made of the Washington County School Association which was formed in 1837. The first officers were William Slocomb, president, Theodore Scott, vice president, Thomas W. Ewart, secretary. At the semi-annual meeting in May, 1838, an address was delivered by Samuel Lewis, Esq., the first State Superintendent of Schools in Ohio. The records of this association show that many of the leading citizens of the county participated in its proceedings, and that many valuable addresses were delivered. The last meeting was held in 1854, prior to which time the school system of the State had been reorganized.

Among the public men to whom the cause of popular education in Ohio was greatly indebted in the early history of the State, none deserves more prominence than Judge Ephraim Cutler. He was a representative in 1819-20, and in 1822-23, and a senator from 1823 to 1825; and his attention was largely devoted to the subjects of equitable taxation and the system of common schools. In 1822 he was appointed by Governor Trimble one of seven commissioners to report a system of education adapted to common schools. In February, 1825, the first general school law was passed by the legislature, providing for a liberal support of schools by general taxation. Mr. Walker, in his History of Athens County, after speaking of Judge Cutler's efforts to reform the system of taxation, says: " His other great achievement at this time was the establishment of an excellent common school system. * * We do not aver that he alone deserves the credit for the success of the measure in the legislature of 1824-25 but he was the acknowledged leader of the friends of common schools, and his experience in public affairs and as a legislator rendered his services of the greatest value."

At different times organizations for mutual improvement have existed, which have called out the efforts of the members and been productive of benefit. A Lyceum was formed in February, 1831, with the following officers: John Cotton, president; Caleb Emerson, vice-president; Arius Nye, corresponding secretary; James M. Booth, recording secretary; John Mills, treasurer; Arius Nye, S. P. Hildreth, curators. Before this Lyceum various lectures were delivered; among others by Dr. John Cotton, Dr. S. P. Hildreth, John Delafield, Jr., Wm. A. Whittlesey, John Brough. About ten years

Libraries and Newspapers.

later another lyceum was formed which was very well sustained for a considerable period. Dr. Cotton gave lectures on Mesmerism, Hon. Arius Nye on Banking, and gentlemen connected with the college lectured on various subjects.

As early as 1810 the Fearing Library Society was incorporated. The act of incorporation named Thomas Stanley, Robert Baird, and Elisha Allen as directors; John Miller as treasurer; and Daniel G. Stanley as librarian. The Society was limited to three thousand dollars of property besides books, maps, and charts.

The Marietta Library was formed, and books purchased, in 1829, and an act of incorporation obtained February 9th, 1830. The corporators named were John Cotton, John Mills, Anselm T. Nye, Samuel P. Hildreth, and Daniel H. Buell. The corporation was restricted in clear annual income to two thousand dollars, and it was provided that none of the funds should "ever be applied to the purposes of banking." This library has been in operation to the present time, and for most of the period has been kept in the brick building on Front street, which was erected by the library company. The number of books is over 3,000.

The first newspaper published in the county was the *Ohio Gazette and the Territorial and Virginia Herald*, printed by Wyllys Silliman, and edited by Elijah Backus. It was first issued in December, 1801. (The third number of the first volume bears the date January 1st, 1802).[1] Mr. Silliman within two years sold the paper to Mr. Backus, and he soon after sold to Fairlamb and Gates. In 1805 Samuel Fairlamb purchased it and changed the name to *Ohio Gazette and*

---

[1]. In the library of the Antiquarian Society at Worcester, Mass.

Virginia Herald. (Volume 1, No. 47 is dated April 24th, 1806).[1] He probably continued it, though somewhat irregularly, till 1810.

The *Western Spectator* was established October 23d, 1810. It was printed by Joseph Israel for Caleb Emerson. In December, 1811, Thomas G. Ransom became the publisher, Mr. Emerson continuing as editor. This paper was published for about two years and a half, and then sold to the proprietors of the *American Friend.*

The first number of the *Friend* was issued April 24th, 1813. It was edited by David Everett, and printed by T. G. Ransom for D. Everett, T. Buell, and D. H. Buell. Mr. Everett died December 21st, of that year. He was the author of the lines beginning

> You'd scarce expect one of my age
> To speak in public on the stage.

Mr. D. H. Buell became the editor January 1st, 1814. In April of that year Royal Prentiss appears as one of the publishers. The number for March 15th, 1816, Vol. 3, No. 27, appeared as Vol. 1, No. 1, New Series, printed by Royal Prentiss. With the first number of Vol. 8, June 26th, 1823, the name was changed to *American Friend and Marietta Gazette,* printed and published by R. & G. Prentiss. Vol. 11, No. 1, has R. Prentiss as printer and publisher, and the paper was so continued to Vol. 17, No. 21, May 11th, 1833. Mr. Prentiss went into the printing office in 1801, and worked on the first number of the first paper.

In 1833 the paper was purchased by John Delafield, Jr. and Edward W. Nye, and was called the *Marietta Gazette.* In 1836 it was under the editorial charge of Mr. Caleb Emerson. In December, 1837, it was pur-

---

1. In the library at Worcester, Mass.

chased by Isaac Maxon. Prior to its union with the *Intelligencer* in 1842, Mr. Edmund B. Flagg was for a while connected with it.

The first number of the *Marietta Intelligencer* appeared August 29th, 1839, edited by Beman Gates, and published by G. W. & C. D. Tyler. In 1842 the Marietta Gazette was purchased and consolidated with the Intelligencer. In 1844 G. W. Tyler and B. Gates were the publishers, and in 1845 Mr. Gates became sole publisher as well as editor. A tri-weekly edition was started October 11th, 1851, and was continued to January 3d, 1861. In April, 1856, T. L. Andrews became the publisher and editor, conducting it till 1862, when it was purchased by Rodney M. Stimson. Mr. Stimson changed the name to *Marietta Register*, and conducted the paper till 1872. Mr. E. R. Alderman became the proprietor in that year, and is still the publisher. The *Register* claims to be the successor of the *Ohio Gazette and Virginia Herald*, and so to have been established in 1801; having thus had, though under different names, a continuity of life for more than three quarters of a century.

There have been various other papers published in the county at different times.

The Commentator and Marietta Recorder was started September 16th, 1807, by James B. Gardiner. In August, 1808, it was called simply *The Commentator;* and in June, 1809, Israel and Gardiner appear as the printers and publishers. It was continued for two or three years, and in politics was opposed to the party then in power.

The Marietta Minerva appeared in October, 1823, published by John K. and A. V. D. Joline. It was suspended in November, 1824. The paper advocated the claims of Henry Clay to the presidency.

The Marietta and Washington County Pilot, by George Dunlevy and A. V. D. Joline, was first issued April 7th, 1826. At first neutral in politics, it espoused the cause of Andrew Jackson in August, 1824. The last number was in May, 1830.

The Western Republican and Marietta Advertiser was started January 8th, 1831, by John Brough before he was twenty years of age. In 1833 he removed the paper to Parkersburg, Virginia, and a few months later to Lancaster, Ohio.

The Marietta Democrat, by Charles B. Flood, appeared in August, 1835. It was published for about two years.

The Washington County Democrat was started in April, 1840, by Daniel Radebaugh, Jr., continuing, however, but for a short time.

The Marietta Republican was first issued November 28th, 1849, Amos Layman, editor. In 1853 A. W. McCormick became the proprietor, Mr. L. continuing a year as associate editor. In 1858 Mr. McC. sold to A. J. Campbell & Co., A. O. Wagstaff becoming the editor. In February, 1860, W. Scott became proprietor, with McCormick editor till October, 1861, then C. Rhodes till its discontinuance in November, 1863.

The *Home News*, a small paper in quarto form, was commenced by E. Winchester, January 1st, 1859. In 1862 it was sold to Mr. Stimson and merged in the *Register*.

The *Marietta Times* was established by Walter C. Hood, the first number having been issued September 24th, 1864. Since August 1st, 1871, it has been owned and edited by S. M. McMillen.

Taxation of Land. 59

The first German paper in this part of the State was established by William Lorey, August 3d, 1856, the *Marietta Demokrat*, which was continued for nine years.

The *Marietta Zeitung* was started by E. Winchester in the fall of 1868. Since March, 1869, it has been published by Jacob Mueller.

In February, 1825, a measure was carried through the legislature, which was closely connected with the financial interests of the State, and especially this part of it. Prior to the admission of Ohio into the Union a law had been published by the Governor and Judges of the Territory, dividing the unimproved land into three classes for the purposes of taxation. This division of the land into first, second, and third classes continued till 1825, and operated very injuriously to the interests of this portion of the State. A public meeting was held at Marietta, December 28th, 1816, to call the attention of the legislature to this unequal taxation. It was asserted that land in Hamilton County, worth $50.00 an acre, was taxed no higher than land in this county, worth fifty cents. A committee was appointed to memorialize the legislature, consisting of Paul Fearing, G. Turner, Nahum Ward, W. R. Putnam, and D. H. Buell.

In the winter of 1819-20, Judge Ephraim Cutler, a representative from this county, introduced into the legislature a joint resolution that property should be taxed according to its true value, which passed the House of Representatives. In the fall of 1823 he was elected to the Senate, and renewed his efforts to secure a reform in the revenue system. He was appointed the chairman of the committee on the revenue. The projec

of a canal between Lake Erie and the Ohio river had
come up and Judge Cutler succeeded in convincing the
friends of that measure that it must inevitably fail unless
based upon a broad, judicious, and equitable system of
taxation. To him more than to any other are we indebted for the law then enacted. The language of his
contemporaries clearly shows that he was regarded as
the author.

Hon. Samuel F. Vinton writes from Washington,
December 21st, 1824: "We ought to offer up our most
unceasing prayers that your plan for the equalization of
taxes may be at the same time adopted. Without it
inevitable ruin would await the sparse-peopled and
sterile parts of the State. In fact those parts of the
State will be virtually ruined under the present system
of taxation in defraying the ordinary expenses of the
government.

Ingenuity, in my opinion, could not devise a system more unequal, unjust, and oppressive. I am de-
cidedly in favor of improving the inland navigation of
the State by canals, if possible; but I hope you will
perseveringly press upon the legislature your plan of
taxation in conjunction with it."

The " Act establishing an equitable mode of levy-
ing taxes of this State," was passed February 3d, 1825;
and an "Act to provide for the internal improvement
of the State of Ohio by navigable Canals," February
4th, 1825.

There were no mail arrangements here till 1794,
and of course no post-office. On the 24th of May of
that year the Postmaster-General, Timothy Pickering,
writes to General R. Putnam: "It is proposed to at-
tempt the carriage of a mail from Pittsburg to Wheel-

ing by land, and thence by water to Limestone (now Maysville). From Limestone by a new road on the southern side of the Ohio to the mouth of Licking, opposite to Fort Washington. * * Marietta will be a station for the boats to stop at as they pass; and doubtless it will be convenient to have a post-office there. Herewith I send a packet addressed to you, to be put into the hands of the person you judge most suitable for postmaster." The person selected by General Putnam was Return Jonathan Meigs, Jr. The fitness of the selection is shown in the fact that twenty years later this deputy postmaster became the Postmaster-General of the United States, which office he held for nine years.

In the same letter General Putnam was requested to select a postmaster for Gallipolis also, which he did. In January, 1795, Colonel Pickering requested General P. to take the whole management of this arrangement from Wheeling to Fort Washington (Cincinnati). He writes: "I am solicitous to commit the whole business to your direction."

The mail was first carried to Zanesville in 1798. Daniel Convers was the contractor, and the schedule required the mail to "leave Marietta every Thursday at one o'clock, P. M., arrive at Zanes Town next Monday at eight o'clock, P. M. Returning, leave Zanes Town every Tuesday at six o'clock, A. M., and arrive at Marietta on Wednesday at six o'clock, P. M." (The schedule and the filling up of the contract are in the handwriting of the Postmaster-General, Joseph Habersham).

The citizens of the county have had broad views as to public improvements. The letter of General Putnam to General Washington in 1783 showed careful study of the subject of routes of travel and transportation.

In 1804, when measures were agitated in Congress for a road from the seaboard to the Ohio river, a committee of gentlemen issued a circular showing reasons for bringing the road to a point opposite Marietta. The circular is signed by R. J. Meigs, Jr., Joseph Buell, Rufus Putnam, Matthew Backus, David Putnam, Benj. I. Gilman, Paul Fearing and Dudley Woodbridge.

In 1831 a letter, signed by S. P. Hildreth, Arius Nye, A. V. D. Joline, Augustus Stone, and Levi Barber, was addressed to Judge Cutler, requesting him to prepare a statement as to a road from Winchester to the Ohio river, to be laid before the legislature of Virginia.

A public meeting was held at the court-house January 3d, 1835, to consider the question of the improvement of the Muskingum river, and a memorial was prepared and laid before the legislature. A bill was introduced the following winter by Isaac Humphries, representative from this county, ordering the work and appropriating $400,000 for the purpose. The bill passed the House February 5th, and the Senate March 4th.

In 1837 a committee appointed at a county meeting commissioned Judge Cutler to go to Baltimore to confer with Mr. McLane, the president of the Baltimore and Ohio Railroad, with regard to the route of that road, which had then been built about eighty miles. The letter to Judge C. bears the signatures of Nahum Ward, Caleb Emerson, John Mills, David Barber, Augustus Stone, and Joseph Barker.

These early efforts show the active interest felt by our citizens in the works of public improvement. It is not necessary to call attention to what Washington county men have done for railroads in Ohio. It was

Flour Mills and Ship-building

their energy that carried through the road to Cincinnati against obstacles that seemed insurmountable. Messrs. W. P. Cutler, N. L. Wilson, John Mills, Douglas Putnam, Beman Gates, and Wm. S. Nye were connected with the road, some of them from its beginning. The Hocking Valley road was projected in good part by Marietta men, and we all know the energy which General A. J. Warner has exerted in pushing forward the Marietta, Pittsburg and Cleveland road.

The first flour mills in Ohio were on Wolf Creek about a mile from its mouth, erected in 1789, by Col. Robert Oliver, Major Haffield White, and Captain John Dodge. Mills were commenced soon after on Duck Creek by Enoch Shepherd with Colonel E. Sproat and Thomas Stanley, but the Indian war and the flood interrupted. In 1798 a floating mill was built five miles up the Muskingum by Captain Jonathan Devol, which, says Dr. Hildreth, for some years did nearly all the grinding for the inhabitants on the Ohio and Muskingum for fifty miles above and below the mill. The "Marietta Steam Mill" (in Harmar), was completed in 1811.

The first tannery was established by Colonel Ichabod Nye in 1791. In 1813 a cotton factory was built for a company, of which William Woodbridge, Joseph Holden, and S. P. Hildreth were directors. Dr. N. McIntosh was the contractor, and his son, our venerable fellow citizen Colonel E. S. McIntosh, says, he himself laid the brick. The building was on Putnam street, between Fourth and Fifth, and twenty years after was converted into the old "Academy."

Ship-building was commenced at Marietta in 1801 by B. I. Gilman. It was prosecuted by him and others with vigor and success till the passage of the embargo act in December, 1807. Marietta suffered greatly in consequence of that measure. "No town in the United States suffered so much in proportion to its capital," (Hildreth). This branch of business was afterwards revived, and ships and steamboats have been built. About thirty years ago some eight or ten ocean vessels were built here; one of which, the "John Farnum," built by A. B. & I. R. Waters, was sent to Ireland with a cargo of corn in charge of Asa B. Waters.

In January, 1829, Dobbins and McElfresh started an iron foundry, called the "Washington Foundry," a little north of the Steam Mill in Harmar. A year later it was bought by A. T. Nye. A few years since the foundry was moved to the building erected for a woolen factory, where it is still carried on by A. T. Nye & Son. The foundry of Mr. Owen Franks, on Second street, was established about 1840 by Franks & Hendrie.

Efforts to establish cotton and woolen manufactures at Marietta have not been very successful though at Beverly there are woolen establishments in a prosperous condition.

While it is difficult to see why these and other manufactures should not flourish here, the best success thus far has been attained in the departments of iron and wood. There have been various foundries and machine-shops, and establishments for the manufacture of buckets and tubs have given employment to many persons. The largest establishment in the place at present is the Marietta Chair Company, of which John Mills is president.

For Agricultural statistical purposes the State is divided into three districts: northern, central and southern,

Statistics—Agriculture and Petroleum.

the latter embracing twenty-two counties. Taking the statistics of the last six years reported, 1869-1874, Washington county holds the eighth place in the number of bushels of wheat raised to the acre—ranging from the eleventh place in 1873 to the fifth in 1874. The yield in 1873 was 9.13 bushels to the acre, and in 1874 it was 13.85. Thus in 1874—the last year whose statistics have been received–of the twenty-two counties, four had a higher average to the acre, and seventeen had a lower; and our county was 14 per cent. above the average of the district.

There is one product in which this county has decided pre-eminence—petroleum. For the years 1873, 1874, the Secretary of State reports for Washington county an aggregate of 2,209,928 gallons, and for the rest of the State 185,280 gallons. Thus this county produces about twelve times as much petroleum as all the other counties combined. From statements kindly furnished by gentlemen engaged in the oil trade the whole production may be given as follows: Cow Run, 510,000 barrels; Macksburgh, 104,000; Newell's Run, Pawpaw, and Fifteen Mile, 6,000; total 620,000 barrels. At three dollars a barrel, the probable average price, we have $1,860,000, as the value of the oil product for about sixteen years. A few of the wells at Macksburgh are over the Noble county line, but the result will not be much diminished.

In a brief account of this county published at New York in 1834, by John Delafield, Jr., mention is made of petroleum—called "spring oil," or "seneca oil,"— as having been known to the hunters and early inhabitants of the county since its first settlement. "It can be used," he says, "in lamps as it affords a brilliant light. It is very useful and therefore much employed in curing the diseases of and injuries done to horses. It is perhaps the best substance known for the prevention of friction in machinery." Most of the oil used by druggists through the different States is sold by a Marietta firm—Bosworth, Wells & Co. This, which is a heavy oil, comes principally from the neighborhood of Hughes river in West Virginia.

An Agricultural Society was formed in 1819, April 28th, styled " The Agricultural and Manufacturing Society of Washington and Wood¹ Counties." The first meeting for the choice of officers was appointed for November 10th, and Ephraim Cutler, Joseph Barker, and Alexander Henderson were appointed to issue an address to the people of the two counties. The meeting was held at the court-house, but was adjourned to the 17th, at the academy. At this adjourned meeting, of which Paul Fearing was chairman and Dr. S. P. Hildreth clerk, the following officers were chosen; Benjamin I. Gilman, president; Christian Schultz, 1st vice-president; Wm. R. Putnam, 2d vice-president; S. P. Hildreth, recording secretary; Nahum Ward, corresponding secretary; David Putnam, treasurer. The board of managers consisted of the president and vice-president, *ex-officio*, with Ebenezer Battelle, George Neale, John Griffith, Ephraim Cutler, J. B. Regnier, Benjamin Dana, A. W. Putnam, Paul Fearing, A. Henderson.

It is probable that from that time to the present the county has not been without an organization for these general purposes. In 1826 a county fair was held; the committee of arrangements being Nahum Ward, S. P. Hildreth, and John Mills, with Joseph Barker, Jr., pres-

---

1. Wood County in Virginia.

Agricultural and Mechanical Association.

sident, and W. B. Barnes, secretary. In June 1834, the county commissioners voted the sum of fifty dollars to the Agricultural Society "to buy seed wheat from New York."

The present organization was made in 1846, since which time the records are complete. The following gentlemen have been presidents: for 1846, Joseph Barker; 1847, George Dana; 1848, Joseph Barker; 1849, William R. Putnam, Jr.; 1850, George W. Barker; 1851, William Devol; 1852, Seth Woodford; 1853, 1854, George W. Barker; 1855-1857, A. B. Battelle; 1858, 1859, L. J. P. Putnam; 1860, George W. Barker; 1861-1867, George Dana, Jr.; 1868, John Newton; 1869, Augustine Dyar; 1870, John D. Barker; 1871, William F. Curtis; 1872, 1873, John Newton; 1874, William R. Putnam, (declined); 1875, 1876, Thomas W. Moore; 1877, P. B. Buell; 1878, Pemberton Palmer.

The society has occupied the present grounds a little more than twenty years. Before that time the court-house served as the floral hall, and the streets adjacent, or some convenient vacant lots, were used for the display of stock. In 1852 subscriptions were commenced for the purchase of grounds and the erection of buildings. Subsequently a company of gentlemen made the purchase, and transferred to the society when a sufficient sum had been raised.

The large mineral resources with which this county abounds have scarcely begun to be developed. It may be that the region included in the purchase by the Ohio Company will prove to be more valuable on account of its mineral wealth than any fertility of soil could make it.

The Bank of Marietta was chartered February 10th, 1808. This was the first bank incorporated as such in the State. (The Miami Exporting Company, incorporated in 1803, exercised banking powers.) The directors named in the act were Rufus Putnam, president, Benjamin Ives Gilman, William Skinner, Paul Fearing, Dudley Woodbridge, Earl Sproat, and David Putnam. The charter was for ten years, but in 1816 the time was extended to January 1st, 1843. The presidents in succession after General Putnam were B. I. Gilman, D. Woodbridge, Levi Barber, and John Mills. The cashiers were David Putnam, David S. Chambers, Alexander Henderson, Benjamin P. Putnam, Wm. B. Barnes, Arius Nye, and Anselm T. Nye.

The State Bank of Ohio was chartered in 1845, and a branch was established at Marietta. John Mills, Noah L. Wilson, and Douglas Putnam, were the successive presidents, and N. L. Wilson, J. R. Crawford, and Israel R. Waters, the cashiers. In 1863 this bank became the Marietta National, with Douglas Putnam, president, and I. R. Waters, cashier. Afterwards Mr. Waters became president and F. E. Pearce, cashier. It is now a private bank.

The First National Bank of Marietta was organized in 1863, with Beman Gates, president, who still holds the office. William F. Curtis was the first cashier, and subsequently Daniel P. Bosworth, and Edward R. Dale.

The First National Bank of Beverly, was started in 1863. Its presidents have been George Bowen, Wm. McIntosh, E. S. McIntosh; the cashiers, Wm. McIntosh, S. R. McIntosh, C. W. Reynolds. This is now a private bank.

The first and only Savings Bank in the county was

Money and Accounts.

established January, 1872—The Dime Savings Society—with John L. Mills, president. W. H. Johnson, treasurer.

It is interesting to note the usages of the pioneers as to money terms and the mode of keeping accounts. In 1785 the Continental Congress had established the decimal system, with the dollar as the unit, and in 1786 they provided for the issue of the gold eagle and half-eagle. While the terms used by the Governor and Judges in the laws were restricted to our decimal notation, the people were slow to give up the pounds, shillings, and pence; and the first fifteen or twenty years after 1788 show a great variety of customs. An account made out by D. Woodbridge, Jr., & Co., in 1799, is in the English currency, and an account book of Joshua Shipman, extending from 1796 to February, 1804, is also in pounds, shillings, and pence. The very last entry shows a change. "Nathan McIntosh, Dr. to 23½ days of the boy James, 23.50." The dollar was equal to six shillings, unless otherwise specified.

A curious use of the decimal system appears in the inventory of the effects of the estate of General Varnum, made January 24th, 1789, by Winthrop Sargent, Charles Greene, and Isaac Pierce, appraisers. The sums are entered in five columns, headed E. D. d. c. m. Thus, one item is - - - $\frac{D \quad d \quad c \quad m}{1 \quad 3 \quad 3 \quad 3}$
Another is - - - - - $\frac{E \quad D \quad d \quad c}{1 \quad 4 \quad 7 \quad 6}$
We should write the two sums $1.33⅓ and $14.76. A bill of Dr. Thos. Farley against General V's estate is "D 16 8 2, ($16.82)." In 1789 a fine of "six dimes and six cents," with costs of " one dollar and five dimes," was imposed for failure in road work. And in the same year the fine and costs of two others were "three dollars and thirty-six ninetieths." A bill of lumber

sold to General Putnam by John White amounted to "9 dollars 90/100." The same mode of reckoning is found in a paper of General Putnam's, drawn up in 1780, when he was in the army.

The following extract is worthy of quotation at a time when the various forms of money, and the values it represents, are so much discussed. It is from a law enacted in 1792 by Winthrop Sargent, acting governor, and John Cleves Symmes and Rufus Putnam, judges, regulating the fees of public officers. "And whereas a dollar varies in its real value in the several counties of the territory, some provision in kind ought to be made, therefore: *Be it enacted:* That for every cent allowed by this act one quart of Indian corn may be demanded and taken by the person to whom the fee is coming, as an equivalent for the cent, always at the election of the person receiving the same, whether to accept of his fee in Indian corn or in specie, at the sum affixed by the foregoing table of fees; one quart of Indian corn being always equal to one cent and so at that rate for a greater or a less sum."

It has been seen that Mr. Joshua Shipman in 1804 charged one dollar a day for his boy James, (at carpenter work). In 1808 the county commissioners ordered that the judges and clerks of the presidential election should receive twenty-five cents a day.

The citizens of this county have not been slow to respond to calls for military service, as is shown by their history from the time of the Indian wars of the last century, down to the great rebellion of 1861-1865. Some of the original papers of enlistment are still in existence, with the signatures of those who volunteered in December, 1806, at the call of the Governor of Ohio to aid in suppressing the Burr insurrection; of those

Military Record.

who responded to the call of President Jefferson for 100,000 men in August, 1807; and of those who volunteered in the war with England 1812-14. The name of Captain Timothy Buell appears on each of these occasions, and in the war with England we find the names of Major Alexander Hill, Captain John Thorniley, Captain E. B. Dana, and Captain J. Ford.

In the late civil war this county furnished over four thousand men, as stated by General T. C. H. Smith in his address at the dedication of the Soldiers' Monument. Besides the many gallant men that went directly from the county, there were in the Union army many others, descendants of the early settlers of Marietta. Among those who held high command were Generals John Pope, Irwin McDowell, and D. C. Buell, who were severally the grandsons of Elijah Backus, Abner Lord, and Timothy Buell.

Such is a brief outline of the history of Washington county. Personal incidents could not be dwelt upon, and there was the less occason as so many have been preserved in the valuable works of the late Dr. S. P. Hildreth. The materials for a full history of the county are abundant, and its preparation should not longer be delayed.

While this county cannot claim pre-eminence in any of the great departments of human industry, yet from the 7th of April, 1788 to the present time there has been no lack of intelligent, capable men in the various vocations of life. High intelligence has been a characteristic from the beginning. None of the villages in the best parts of New England could show a larger proportion of liberally educated men than Marietta, Belpre, and Waterford, in the first twenty years of their history. And within the present generation the public spirit and intelligent liberality of some of the citizens of this place have made their names and the name of Marietta household words in the best circles of the land.

In early times many came to Marietta to sojourn for a while and from here went out to their permanent homes. This was their temporary residence; and pleasant recollections of it and its inhabitants seem always to have remained with them. So now we often meet with those who have made Marietta a place of educational sojourn; who have spent here a portion of their youth in intellectual training, and have then gone forth to do the work assigned them. But, unlike those who in the early days made this the gateway to the great west, and who have now all passed away, their number will increase year by year. Even now you will find them scattered from Maine to Georgia, from Texas to Oregon. Whatever may be the future of this town as a mart of trade or a manufacturing point, there is every probability that it will become more and more an important educational center. In beauty of situation and the intelligence and refinement of its people it can compare favorably with the most noted seats of learning, while the remarkable generosity of the founders and friends of the College cannot fail to stimulate others here and elsewhere to provide the means for its continued increase in efficiency and usefulness.

May the people of Washington county be prospered in all that pertains to their highest well-being. May her future, for the next century, and for all coming centuries, be worthy of the noble men who here laid the foundations of this State and the great north-west— worthy of the illustrious citizen whose name the county bears.

APPENDIX.

Lists of the various Civil Officers have been prepared, and are appended to the discourse. These embrace the judges of the Territory, judges of the Court of Common Pleas, members of Congress, senators and representatives in the General Assembly, postmasters at Marietta, and the various county officers.

APPENDIX.

JUDGES OF THE TERRITORY.

The Territorial Court was composed of three Judges, appointed at first by Congress, and afterwards by the President. John Armstrong and William Barton were appointed but declined. The following is the list with the dates of appointment:

Samuel H. Parsons......................Oct. 16, 1787..Nov. 17, 1789: died.
James M. Varnum.....................Oct. 16, 1787..Jan. 10, 1789: died.
John Cleves Symmes ....Feb. 19, 1788..1803: State formed.
George Turner..........................Sept. 12, 1789..1798: resigned.
Rufus Putnam..........................Mar. 31, 1790..Dec. 22, 1796: resigned.
Joseph Gilman ....Dec. 22, 1796..1803: State formed.
Return J. Meigs, Jr....................Feb. 12, 1798..1803, State formed.

COURT OF COMMON PLEAS.

Such a court existed prior to the State; it was composed of not less than three nor more than five judges. The following gentlemen were judges, though their exact terms of service cannot be given.

Rufus Putnam, Benjamin Tupper, Archibald Crary, Joseph Gilman Dudley Woodbridge, Robert Oliver, Daniel Loring, John G. Petit, Isaac Pierce, Griffin Greene, Ephraim Cutler, Peregrine Foster.

The constitution of 1802 provided for a Court of Common Pleas to consist of one president judge and two or three associate judges, all to be appointed by the legislature and to hold office for seven years. There were to be three president judges for the State, but the associate judges were appointed in each county.

PRESIDENT JUDGES FOR THE CIRCUIT.

Calvin Pease..........1803..1808
William Wilson......1808..1819
Ezra Osborne........1819..1826
Thomas Irwin........1826..1840

John E. Hanna, ...1840..1847
Arius Nye,..............1847..1850
Archibald G. Brown..1850..1852

ASSOCIATE JUDGES FROM 1803 to 1852.

Griffin Greene ....1803..1808
Joseph Buell....................1803..1810
Joseph Wood ....1803..1808
Ezekiel Deming..............1808..1824
William Hempstead........1808..1810
Paul Fearing ....1810..1817
Thomas Lord..................1810..1817
Henry Jolly ....1817..1824
John Sharp....................1817..1823
Judah M. Chamberlain....1823..1824

Walter Curtis..................1824..1837
Henry P. Wilcox ....1824..1825
Anaxamander Warner ......1824..1830
John Cotton..................1825..1847
Joseph Barker ....1830..1843
Oliver R. Loring............1837..1847
Isaac Humphreys ....1843..1843
Ebenezer Gates...............1843..1844
Joseph Barker, Jr.............1844..1852
Bial Steadman................1847..1852

William R. Putnam, Jr..............1847..1852.

Appendix.

By the constitution of 1851 the State for judicial purposes is divided into districts and sub-districts. A judge is elected in each sub-district for five years. This county is united with Gallia, Meigs and Athens, constituting the third sub-district of the seventh district. Since 1868 there have been two judges in this sub-district.

JUDGES OF THE COURT OF COMMON PLEAS FROM 1852.

Simeon Nash ....1852..1862	David B. Hebard, Jan. 1875..Oct. '75
John Welch ....1862..1865	John Cartwright, Feb. 1875..Oct. '75
Erastus A. Guthrie..........1865..1874	J. P. Bradbury, Oct. 1875..Feb. '77
William B. Loomis ....1868..1873	Sam'l S. Knowles, Oct. 1875..Feb. '78
Tobias A. Plants..............1873..1875	J. P. Bradbury, Feb. 1877..Feb. '82
Samuel S. Knowles,......Feb. 1878..Feb. 1883	

Judge Welch was elected to the Supreme Court, Judges Guthrie and Plants resigned, and Judges Hebard and Cartwright were appointed by the Governor. Judges Bradbury and Knowles are the present incumbents.

PROBATE JUDGES.

A Probate Court was established in the first year of the Territory, the Governor appointing the judge. The first state constitution abolished the court, but the second restored it. The judge is elected by the people for three years.

Rufus Putnam.............................Oct. 1788..Dec. 1789, (resigned.)
Joseph Gilman........ ....Dec. 1789..Dec. 1796, (resigned.)
Paul Fearing ....Mar. 1797..Mar. 1803.
Thomas W. Ewart......................Feb. 1852..Oct. 1852, (resigned.)
Davis Green...................................Oct. 1852..Feb. 1855.
William Devol..............................Feb. 1855..Feb. 1858.
Charles R. Rhodes.......................Feb. 1858..Feb. 1861.
Charles F. Buell...........................Feb. 1861..Feb. 1864.
Luman W. Chamberlain..............Feb. 1864..Feb. 1870.
A. W. McCormick.......................Feb. 1870..Feb. 1876.
C. T. Frazyer ....Feb. 1876..Feb. 1879.

COURT OF GENERAL QUARTER SESSIONS OF THE PEACE.

Such a court was established in 1788, and was continued in each county till 1803. The duties were partly judicial and partly executive. The court established townships, laid out new roads, appointed overseers of the poor for the townships, granted licenses for houses of entertainment, &c.

The following Justices were members of the court at different times: Joseph Gilman, Isaac Pierce, Robert Oliver, Dudley Woodbridge, Josiah Munro, John G. Petit, Griffin Greene, William R. Putnam, Samuel Williamson, Joseph Barker, Ephraim Cutler, Henry Smith, Phillip Whitten, Alvin Bingham, Thomas Stanley, Seth Carhart, Robert Safford, William Harper, William Burnham, Joseph Buell.

MEMBERS OF STATE CONSTITUTIONAL CONVENTIONS.

1802.	1850-51.
Ephraim Cutler,	Thomas W. Ewart,
Benjamin Ives Gilman,	William P. Cutler.
John McIntire,	1873-74.
Rufus Putnam.	Harlow Chapin.

The constitution of 1802 was not submitted to the vote of the people; that of 1874 was rejected by a large majority.

Appendix

MEMBERS OF THE GENERAL ASSEMBLY.

The first election of representatives to the territorial legislature was in 1798. Paul Fearing and Return Jonathan Meigs, Senior, were elected from Washington county. Colonel Robert Oliver was appointed by the President one of the five members of the Council, or upper house, and subsequently became its president. The legislature met for its first session September 16th, 1799; and for its second, November 3d, 1800.

Ephraim Cutler and William R. Putnam were elected representatives to the second legislature, which met November 24th, 1801. These gentlemen were also re-elected in October, 1802, to the third territorial legislature; which, however, was never convened, as Ohio was admitted into the Union February 19th, 1803. Nor did the second legislature hold a second sesssion.

The first State legislature met March 1st, 1803, the second on the first Monday of December, 1803. The senators were elected for two years, the representatives for one. This county has been associated with others in the election of senators, and at times also in the election of representatives. In 1803 and 1804 she elected alone. From 1805 to 1807, inclusive, the district embraced Washington, Gallia, Muskingum, and Athens. From 1808 to 1819, it embraced Washington and Athens; and from 1820 to 1823, Washington and Morgan. Since that time Washington county has constituted the district.

The following list contains the names of those only who belonged in this county, as it is now bounded. Under the first constitution the sessions of the legislature began on the first Monday of December.

TERRITORIAL LEGISLATURE.

SENATORS.	REPRESENTATIVES.
Robert Oliver (President) 1799..1803.	Paul Fearing......⎫ 1799..1801. Return J. Meigs..⎭ Ephraim Cutler......⎫ 1801..1803. William R. Putnam.⎭

STATE LEGISLATURE.

	SENATORS.	REPRESENTATIVES.
1st Assembly	Joseph Buell	William Jackson......1803.
2d "	⎧ Joseph Buell.......... ⎩ Elijah Backus........	William Jackson......1803.
3d "	Joseph Buell	Seth Carhart......1804.
4th "	⎧ Joseph Buell ...... ⎩ Hallam Hempstead.	......1805.
5th "	Hallam Hempstead.	Levi Barber......1806.
6th "	John Sharp	Joseph Palmer......1807.
7th "	John Sharp	William Woodbridge......1808.
8th "		William R. Putnam......1809.
9th "		S. P. Hildreth......⎫ 1810. W. R. Putnam......⎭
10th "	William Woodbridge	S. P. Hildreth......1811.
11th "	William Woodbridge	Sardine Stone......1812.
12th "	William Woodbridge	Sardine Stone......1813.
13th "	William R. Putnam	John Sharp......1814.
14th "	John Sharp	Henry Jolly......1815.
15th "	John Sharp	Sardine Stone......1816.
16th "	Sardine Stone	Nathanael Hamilton......1817.
17th "	Sardine Stone	Joseph Barker......1818.

Appendix.

	SENATORS.	REPRESENTATIVES.	
18th Assembly	......Sardine Stone	Ephraim Cutler......................	1819.
19th "	......Sardine Stone	Timothy Buell........................	1820.
20th "	......Sardine Stone	Timothy Buell........................	1821.
21st "	......Sardine Stone	Ephraim Cutler......................	1822.
22d "	......Ephraim Cutler........	William Skinner.....................	1823.
23d "	......Ephraim Cutler........	John Cotton..........................	1824.
24th "		William R. Putnam................	1825.
25th "		William R. Putnam................	1826.
26th "	......William R. Putnam..	Arius Nye.............................	1827.
27th "	......William R. Putnam..	Arius Nye.............................	1828.
28th "		Joseph Barker, Jr	1829.
29th "		Joseph Barker, Jr	1830.
30th "	......Arius Nye......	James M. Booth....................	1831.
31st "	......Arius Nye......	James M. Booth....................	1832.
32d "		Silas Cook............................	1833.
33d "		Joseph Barker, Jr	1834.
34th "		Isaac Humphreys...................	1835.
35th "		Isaac Humphreys...................	1836.
36th "		Walter Curtis.......................	1837.
37th "		Walter Curtis.......................	1838.
38th "	......Isaac Humphreys ...	William A. Whittlesey............	1839.
39th "	......Isaac Humphreys ...	Arius Nye.............................	1840.
40th "		Truxton Lyon.......................	1841.
41st "		George M. Woodbridge...........	1842.
42d "		William Glines......................	1843.
43d "		William P. Cutler..................	1844.
44th "	......Rufus E. Harte........	William P. Cutler..................	1845.
45th "	......Rufus E. Harte........	William P. Cutler (Speaker)....	1846.
46th "		George W. Barker.................	1847.
47th "		Seth Woodford......................	1848.
48th "	......George W. Barker.	Seth Woodford......................	1849.
49th "	......George W. Barker.	Ebenezer Battelle, Jr...............	1850.

Under the constitution of 1851 both senators and representatives are elected for two years. The regular sessions commence on the first Monday of January.

	SENATORS.	REPRESENTATIVES.	
50th Assembly........		Levi Bartlett..........................	1852.
51st "	Harley Laflin................	Thomas Ross	1854.
52d "	....	Sam'l Hutchinson ⎫ James Lawton ⎭	1856.
53d "	Davis Green................	A. S. Bailey ⎫ O. Lewis Clarke ⎭	1858.
54th "		John Haddow.......................	1860.
55th "		O. Lewis Clarke....................	1862.
56th "	William F. Curtis........	Mark Green..........................	1864.
57th "	Samuel S. Knowles.......	A. L. Curtis ⎫ A. L. Haskin ⎬ James B. Green[1] ⎭	1866.
58th "	....	Sam'l M. Richardson ⎫ Perez B. Buell ⎭	1868.
59th "	Rodney M. Stimson......	John A. Brown	1870.
60th "	Rodney M. Stimson......	William G. Way....................	1872.
61st "	Perez B. Buell.............	John Varley..........................	1874.
62d "	....	Henry Bohl ⎫ Gilbert Smith ⎭	1876.
63d "	John Irvine..................	Henry Bohl ⎫ Gilbert Smith ⎭	1878.

1. Mr. Green was elected to fill the vacancy caused by the death of Mr. Haskin.

Appendix.

MEMBERS OF CONGRESS.

The Territory was represented in Congress by a delegate for four years from 1799 to 1803. Wm. H. Harrison was the first delegate. Having been appointed Governor of the Territory of Indiana, he was succeeded by Wm. McMillan. From 1801 to 1803, Paul Fearing, of this county, was the delegate. From 1803 to 1813 Ohio had but one representative in Congress. From 1813 to 1823 she had six; from 1823 to 1833, fourteen; 1833 to 1843, nineteen; 1843 to 1863, twenty-one; 1863 to 1873, nineteen; since 1873, twenty. Washington county from 1803 has been in the following Congressional districts: first, third, seventh, sixth, thirteenth, sixteenth, fifteenth.

Territory,		William Henry Harrison, Hamilton Co.	1799–1800.
"		William McMillan, Hamilton Co.	1800–1801.
"		Paul Fearing, Washington Co.	1801–1803.
Whole State,		Jeremiah Morrow, Warren Co.	1803–1813.
3d District,		William Creighton, Jr., Ross Co.	1813–1817.
3d	"	Levi Barber, Washington Co.	1817–1819.
3d	"	Henry Brush, Ross Co.	1819–1821.
3d	"	Levi Barber, Washington Co.	1821–1823.
7th	" (10 yrs)	Samuel F. Vinton, Gallia Co.	1823–1837.
6th	" (4 yrs)		
6th	"	Calvary Morris, Athens Co.	1837–1843.
13th	"	Perley B. Johnson, Morgan Co.	1843–1845.
13th	"	Isaac Parrish, Morgan Co.	1845–1847.
13th	"	Thomas Ritchey, Perry Co.	1847–1849.
13th	"	William A. Whittlesey, Washington Co.	1849–1851.
13th	"	James M. Gaylord, Morgan Co.	1851–1853.
16th	"	Edward Ball, Muskingum Co.	1853–1857.
16th	"	Cydnor B. Tompkins, Morgan Co.	1857–1861.
16th	"	William P. Cutler, Washington Co.	1861–1863.
15th	"	James R. Morris, Monroe Co.	1863–1865.
15th	"	Tobias A. Plants, Meigs Co.	1865–1869.
15th	"	Eliakim H. Moore, Athens Co.	1869–1871.
15th	"	William P. Sprague, Morgan Co.	1871–1875.
15th	"	Nelson H. Van Vorhes, Athens Co.	1875–1879.

COUNTY COMMISSIONERS.

Provision was made for three such officers by a law adopted from the Pennsylvania code by the Governor and Judges in 1795, and confirmed by the Territorial legislature in 1799. They were to be appointed by the Court of Quarter Sessions. The State law of 1804 provided for their election by the people, one each year, the term of office being three years.

The following were appointed under the law of the Territory: Wm. R. Putnam, Paul Fearing, Oliver Rice, Gilbert Devol, Jonathan Haskell, Simeon Deming, Isaac Pierce. Of these, Isaac Pierce served till 1804, W. R. Putnam till 1805, and Simeon Deming till 1806. The list of those elected in successive years is as follows:

1804......Nathanael Hamilton	1811......Daniel Goodno
1805......John Sharp	1812......Henry Jolly
1806......Paul Fearing	1813......Nathanael Hamilton
1807......Nathanael Hamilton	1814......Daniel Goodno
1808......Joseph Barker	1815......William Skinner
1809......Paul Fearing (resigned)	1816......Titan Kemble
1809......John Sharp (for 2 yrs)	1817......John B. Regnier
1810......Nathanael Hamilton	1818......Daniel Goodno

Appendix.

1819......Titan Kemble (resigned)	1847......Lewis H. Greene
1820......John B. Regnier (died)	1848......Douglas Putnam
1821......Samuel Beach (2 years)	1849......John Breckenridge
1821......Amzi Stanley (1 year)	1850......George Stanley
1821......Daniel Goodno	1851......Douglas Putnam
1822......Joseph Barker	1852......Walter Curtis
1823......William R. Putnam	1853......Benjamin Rightmire
1824......Daniel H. Buell (resigned)	1854......William Mason
1825......Joseph Barker	1855......Walter Curtis
1825......Thomas White (1 year)	1856......Charles Dana
1826......William Pitt Putnam	1857......William R. Putnam
1826......Silas Cook (1 year)	1858......Joseph Penrose
1827......Anselm T. Nye	1859......Zachariah Cochrane
1828......Seth Baker (1 year)	1860......James McWilliams
1829......Joel Tuttle	1861......J. J. Hollister
1829......Jabish F. Palmer (2 years)	1862......Wm. Thomas
1830......Anselm T. Nye	1863......Anthony Sheets (resigned)
1831......Jabish F. Palmer	1864......J. J. Hollister
1832......Ebenezer Battelle	1856......George Benedict
1833......William Pitt Putnam	1865......James Little (1 year)
1834......John D. Chamberlain	1866......James Little
1835......Robert K. Ewart	1867......Seymour Clough
1836......Daniel H. Buell	1868......George Benedict
1837......John D. Chamberlain	1869......Thomas Caywood
1838......William Dana	1870......Mark Green (resigned)
1839......Daniel H. Buell	1871......Joseph Penrose
1840......John D. Chamberlain	1871......Cyrenius Buchanan (2 years)
1841......James Dutton	1872......John Hall
1842......Douglas Putnam	1873......Pemberton Palmer
1843......Hiram Gard	1874......John Pool
1844......William West	1875......John Potter
1845......Douglas Putnam	1876......Moses A. Maltster
1846......Boylston Shaw	1877......John Hoppel

COUNTY AUDITOR.

The office was created in 1820. The General Assembly appointed the first Auditor. In 1821 the Auditor was required to be elected by the people each year. In 1824 the law made the term two years.

The successive Auditors have been :

Royal Prentiss ....1820..1825	Horatio Booth...............1854..1856
William A. Whittlesey......1825..1838	Frederick A. Wheeler.......1856..1864
James M. Booth...............1838..1840	Zadok G. Bundy.............1864..1868
Joseph P. Wightman......1840..1842	John V. Ramsey.............1868..1870
James M. Booth..............1842..1846	John T. Matthews..,.........1870..1876
Sala Bosworth................1846..1854	Benjamin J. McKinney.....1876..1878

COUNTY RECORDERS.

Under the Territory the Recorder—styled *Register* till 1795—was appointed by the Governor. By the law of 1803 the associate judges appointed, for seven years. By the law of 1829 the people elect, for three years.

Enoch Parsons..1788.........1790
Dudley Woodbridge......................April, 1790..June, 1807
Giles Hempstead.............................June, 1807..June, 1814
George Dunlevy ....June, 1814..June, 1817

Daniel H. Buell............................June, 1817..Oct., 1834
James M. Booth...........................Oct., 1834..Nov. 1837
Daniel P. Bosworth......................Nov., 1837..Oct., 1843
Stephen Newton..........................Oct., 1843..Nov. 1855
William B. Mason........................Nov., 1855..Jan. 1862
Manly Warren.............................Jan., 1862..May, 1864
Wm. Warren (appointed)............May, 1864..Jan. 1865
Geo. J. Bartmess..........................Jan., 1865..Aug. 1866
A. T. Ward (appointed)...............Aug., 1866..Jan. 1867
James Nixon................................Jan., 1867..

COUNTY TREASURERS.

The Governor appointed till the formation of the State. By the law of 1803, the associate judges appointed. By the law of 1804, the commissioners appointed annually. Since 1827 the people have elected, for two years. By the constitution of 1851 the Treasurer is eligible only four years in six.

Jonathan Stone ....1792..1801
Jabez True........................1801..1817
Joseph Holden..................1817..1828
Weston Thomas...............1828..1830
Royal Prentiss..................1830..1832
Michael Deterly...............1832..1836
Ebenezer Gates ....1836..1838
Robert Crawford.............1838..1850
Abner L. Guitteau..........1850..1856

Stephen Newton...............1856..1858
Ebenezer B. Leget............1858..1860
William B. Thomas..........1860..1862
Rufus E. Harte ....1862..1866
William B. Mason............1866..1868
Lewis Anderson...............1868..1870
Ernest Lindner.................1870..1874
William S. Waugh............1874..1878
William R. Goddard........1878..1880

COUNTY COLLECTORS.

For some years prior to 1804 there were township collectors, and they performed some service in 1805. The office of County Collector was abolished in 1827.

Nathanael Cushing............1804..1806
William Burnham............1806..1807
Obadiah Lincoln...............1807..1808

Timothy Buell..................1808..1820
Jesse Loring.....................1820..1822
Timothy Buell..................1822..1823

Jesse Loring..........1823..1827.

SHERIFFS.

Under the Territory the Governor appointed. Under the State the people elect, for two years. Sheriffs are eligible only four years in six.

Ebenezer Sproat.......................Sept. 2, 1788 to   1802
William Skinner......................1802 to   1803
John Clark ....1803 to   1810
William Skinner......................1810 to   1812
Timothy Buell.........................1812 to   1814
Alexander Hill........................1814 to   1816
Timothy Buell........................1816 to Oct. 1820
Silas Cook................................Oct. 1820 to " 1824
Jesse Loring............................ " 1824 to " 1828
Robert R. Green..................... " 1828 to " 1832
Jesse Loring............................ " 1832 to " 1834
Benjamin M. Brown.............. " 1834 to " 1838
John Test................................. " 1838 to " 1842
George W. Barker.................. " 1842 to " 1846
Junia Jennings........................ " 1846 to ,, 1850
Jesse Hildebrand.................... " 1850 to Jan. 1853
Marcellus J. Morse................Jan. 1853 to ,, 1857

Appendix.

Mark Green	" 1857 to "	1861
Augustus Winsor	" 1861 to "	1865
Jackson A. Hicks	" 1865 to "	1869
Samuel L. Grosvenor	" 1869 to "	1873
George Davenport	" 1873 to "	1877
William T. Stedman	" 1877 to "	1879

CORONERS.

Provision was made in 1788 for a Coroner in each county, to be appointed by the Governor. The first State constitution also provided for one to be elected every two years by the people, and a law of 1854 continued the provision. The list appended is believed to be correct from 1812 to the present time; there is some uncertainty as to the previous periods.

Charles Green (Territory).		Chauncey T. Judd	1850
Joel Bowen	1803	Finley Wilson	1852
Joseph Holden	1806	James H. Jones	1853
Alexander Hill	1812	Chauncey T. Judd	1855
Silas Cook	1814	Benjamin F. Stone	1857
Sampson Cole	1816	Louis Soyez	1859
Silas Cook	1818	Allen M. Creigbaum	1860
John Merrill	1820	Lemuel Grimes	1864
Griffin Greene	1824	Simeon D. Hart	1866
Francis Devol	1834	Herman Michaelis	1868
Warden Willis	1836	Philip Emrich	1870
Lawrence Chamberlain	1838	Marcellus J. Morse	1872
John T. Clogston	1844	T. C. Kiger	1874
Lawrence Chamberlain	1846	Conrad Krigbaum	1876

PROSECUTING ATTORNEYS.

This officer was appointed by the courts under the territory. The State law of 1803 gave the appointment to the Supreme Court, and that of 1805 to the Court of Common Pleas. From 1833 the people have elected. The term of office is two years.

Paul Fearing	Sept. 9, 1788 to		1794
Return Jonathan Meigs, Jr.	1794 to		1798
Matthew Backus	1798 to		1808
William Woodbridge	1808 to	Feb. 6,	1815
Caleb Emerson	Feb. 6. 1815 to	April 10,	1821
John P. Mayberry	April 10, 1821 to	Oct. 30,	1829
Arius Nye	Oct. 30, 1829 to	Aug. 17,	1840
David Barber	Oct. 26, 1840 to	April 3,	1845
Arius Nye	April 3, 1845 to	March 8,	1847
William D. Emerson	March 8, 1847 to	March 13,	1848
William S. Nye	March 13, 1848 to	March,	1850
Davis Green	March, 1850 to	April 5,	1852
Rufus E. Harte	April 5, 1852 to	Oct. 4,	1852
Samuel B. Robinson	Oct. 4, 1852 to	Jan.	1855
Charles R. Rhodes	Jan. 1855 to	Jan.	1857
Samuel B. Robinson	Jan. 1857 to	Jan.	1859
Charles R. Barclay	Jan. 1859 to	Jan.	1861
Frank Buell	Jan. 1861 to	April,	1861
Melvin Clarke	April 1861 to	Oct. 11,	1861
William S. Nye	Oct. 11, 1861 to	Jan.	1862
David Alban	Jan. 1862 to	Jan.	1868
Walter Brabham	Jan. 1868 to	Jan.	1870
Reuben L. Nye	Jan. 1870 to	Jan.	1872

Walter Bratham............................Jan. 1872 to Jan.   1874
Samuel B. Robinson....................Jan. 1874 to Jan.   1876
Frank F. Oldham..........................Jan. 1876 to Jan.   1880

CLERKS OF THE COURT OF COMMON PLEAS.

Under the Territory the title for Clerk of the Court of Common Pleas was Prothonotary. This officer and the clerk of the Court of Quarter Sessions were appointed by the Governor. Under the State Constitution of 1802 the Court appointed its own clerk for seven years. Under that of 1851 the people elect, for three years.

Return Jonathan Meigs............Sept. 9, 1798 to June 9,   1795
Benjamin Ives Gilman..............June 9, 1795 to July,   1803
Edward W. Tupper.....................July, 1803 to Oct. 31,   1808
Giles Hempstead ....Oct. 31, 1808 to Jan. 1 1809
Levi Barber................................Jan. 1. 1809 to March 1, 1817
George Dunlevy ....March 1, 1817 to Oct. 31, 1836
Thomas W. Ewart......................Oct. 31, 1836 to Oct. 21, 1851
William C. Taylor.....................Oct 21, 1851 to Feb.   1852
George S. Gilliland....................Feb. 1852 to July,   1852
William C. Taylor.....................July, 1852 to Feb.   1854
O. Lewis Clarke........................Feb. 1854 to Feb.   1857
Jasper S. Sprague......................Feb. 1857 to Feb.   1863
Willis H. Johnson......................Feb. 1863 to Feb.   1866
Jewett Palmer..........................Feb. 1866 to Feb.   1872
Daniel B. Torpy........................Feb. 1872 to Feb.   1878
Christian H. Etz........................Feb. 1878 to Feb.   1881

COUNTY SURVEYORS.

From 1803 to 1831 the surveyor was appointed by the Court of Common Pleas and Commissioned by the Governor Since 1831 the election has been by the people, for three years.

Levi Barber................................Nov. 1805 to July,   1816
William R. Putnam....................July, 1816 to Oct.   1826
William R. Browning................Feb. 1827 to May,   1832
Benj. F. Stone............................May, 1832 to Nov.   1841
Levi Bartlett..............................Nov. 1841 to Oct.   1851
L. W. Chamberlain....................Oct. 1851 to Dec.   1861
R. W. St. John..........................Dec. 1861 to Dec.   1864
Charles E. Gard[1] (appointed).....Jan. 1865 to Dec.   1865
John A. Plumer.........................Feb. 1866 to Jan.   1875
J. P. Hulbert.............................Jan. 1875 to Jan.   1881

INFIRMARY DIRECTORS.

These officers were appointed by the Commissioners from 1836 until 1842, when they were required to be elected by the people, one each year, to serve three years.

Sampson Cole............1836..1842	Brooks Blizzard............1845..1851
Eben Gates................1836..1842	John Collins................1847..1859
Wyllys Hall................1836..1842	James M. Booth..........1849..1850
James Dunn...............1842..1849	James Dunn................1850..1861
Thos. F. Stanley........1842..1844	James Dutton..............1850..1853
Wm. R. Putnam, Jr....1842..1845	James S. Cady............1853..1856
Samuel Shipman........1844..1847	Robert T. Miller..........1854..1860

1. Samuel N. Hobson was elected Oct. 1864, but resigned.

Appendix.

Levi L. Fay	1856..1862	Samuel E. Fay	1868..1871
Robert B. Cheatham	1860..1863	H. W. Corner	1870..1873
Junia Jennings	1861..1870	Charles Athey	1871..1874
John Dowling	1862..1865	Geo. W. Richards	1873..1876
William West	1863..1866	William Caywood, 3d	1874..1880
James Dunn	1865..1868	John Dowling	1875..1878
F. A. Wheeler	1866..1875	Charles A. Cook	1876..1879

TRUSTEES OF THE CHILDENS' HOME.

By the Act of March 20, 1866, five trustees were to be appointed by the County Commissioners, to serve one year each. By the Act of April 10, 1867, the number of trustees was reduced to three, and the term of service extended to three years.

Douglas Putnam	June, 1866	to March, 1868
William R. Putnam	June, 1866	to March, 1877
Frederick A. Wheeler	June, 1866	Incumbent
William S. Ward	June, 1866	to May, 1871
Augustin Dyar	June, 1866	to March, 1868
Wylie H. Oldham	June, 1871	to June, 1875
W. Dudley Devol	Sept. 1875	Incumbent
George Benedict	March, 1877	Incumbent

POSTMASTERS OF MARIETTA.

Return Jonathan Meigs, Jr	May, 1794	to Oct.	1795
Josiah Munro	Oct. 1795	to	1800
David Putnam	1800	to	1802
Griffin Greene	1802	to	1804
Philip Greene	1804	to	1806
Griffin Greene, Jr	1806	to	1815
Samuel Hoit	1816	to	1818
Henry P. Wilcox	1818	to	1825
David Morris	Jan. 1825	to Aug.	1825
Daniel H. Buell	1825	to	1829
A. V. D. Joline	1829	to	1841
A. L. Guitteau	1841	to	1850
F. A. Wheeler	1850	to	1853
Nathanael Bishop	1853	to	1857
A. W. McCormick	1857	to	1861
Sala Bosworth	1861	to	1870
W. B. Mason	1870		

www.ingramcontent.com/pod-product-compliance
Lightning Source LLC
Chambersburg PA
CBHW030347100526
44592CB00010B/860